Hackney:

An Uncommon History in Five Parts

Edited by Margaret Willes

Hackney Society

Contents

Cover, The Olympic Park. (Grant Smith, www.grant-smith.com)

Frontispiece, Interior of the abandoned German Hospital in the 1990s, before gentrification. (Glory Hall)

Left, The Premier Skating Rink in Clapton, *c.*1912. (Hackney Archives)

Inside back cover, The Horse and Groom, by the River Lea, engraving 1830. (Hackney Archives)

The Hackney Society works to preserve Hackney's unique heritage and make the area a better place in which to live and work. Formed in 1967 it seeks to involve and support local people in the regeneration and conservation of Hackney's built environment and open spaces. We aim to promote high standards of planning, architecture and conservation in Hackney; give a voice to local people in the future development of the borough; and educate and foster public interest in the history, architecture and character of Hackney.

The Society meets monthly for a programme of walks, tours and talks about Hackney's modern and historic buildings; publishes books, newsletters and walks on that subject; organises special community projects; and comments on planning applications.

The Hackney Society is a membership organisation and is a registered charitable company. An elected board of trustees, drawn from the membership, manages the work of the Society. The Hackney Society is a civic and amenity society.

Published in 2012 by
The Hackney Society
The Round Chapel
1d Glenarm Road
London E5 0LY

info@hackneysociety.org
www.hackneysociety.org

Edited by Margaret Willes

Editorial assistants: Frances Elks and Helen King
Designed by Design@GloryHall.com

ISBN 978-0-9536734-2-1

Editor's Foreword

The idea for this book came from Ann Robey. This proved irresistible, though the schedule was terrifying, given the deadline presented by the London 2012 Olympics. It is a tribute to the contributors that the book has come to fruition, especially as they have all provided their texts without remuneration. The Hackney Society is deeply grateful to them.

This is not a conventional history of Hackney, nor is it intended to be comprehensive. The authors have been given *carte blanche* to choose what they considered the defining aspects of the three parishes of Hackney, Stoke Newington and Shoreditch at a particular date, the retrospective anniversaries of the 2012 Olympics. Although buildings come into the story, especially those that can still be seen and sometimes visited, it is the people who occupy centre stage. And what a fascinating cast of characters they have proved. Thomas Sutton, for instance, whose penny-pinching mode of living resulted in one of the most generous bequests of the Jacobean age. Dudley Ryder, son of a dissenting Hackney linen draper, who kept a frank diary worthy of comparison to Samuel Pepys, chronicling the life of the village in the early 18th century. Anna Laetitia Barbauld, another dissenter, who brought her literary career to an end in 1812 when she prophesied that the British Empire would have to make way for the rising power of the United States of America. Marie Lloyd, one of the great music-hall stars of the turn of the last century, with her risqué songs and scandalous lifestyle.

It is our hope, with this 'uncommon history', to entertain not only those who live in the borough or are familiar with its great variety of people and places, but also those who are brought here for the first time with the events of the Games.

People have been very generous with their support. First of all we are very grateful to Edward Benyon, the trustees of the Benyon Estate and Macdonald Wright Architects for giving us funds to enable this book to be published. Hackney Archives, reopening just in time, have been helpful and generous in the supply of pictures, and I would particularly like to thank Elizabeth Green. Grant Smith moved with lightning speed to take the very fine photograph on the front cover. Thanks also to Laurie Elks, Patrick Hammill, Hannah Parham, Stephen Selby, Holly Stout, Daniel Betts, Jean Field, Jane Howe and Julia Lafferty. Lastly, thanks must go to Glory Hall who has coped with the design and production, remaining calm throughout the hectic schedule.

Margaret Willes

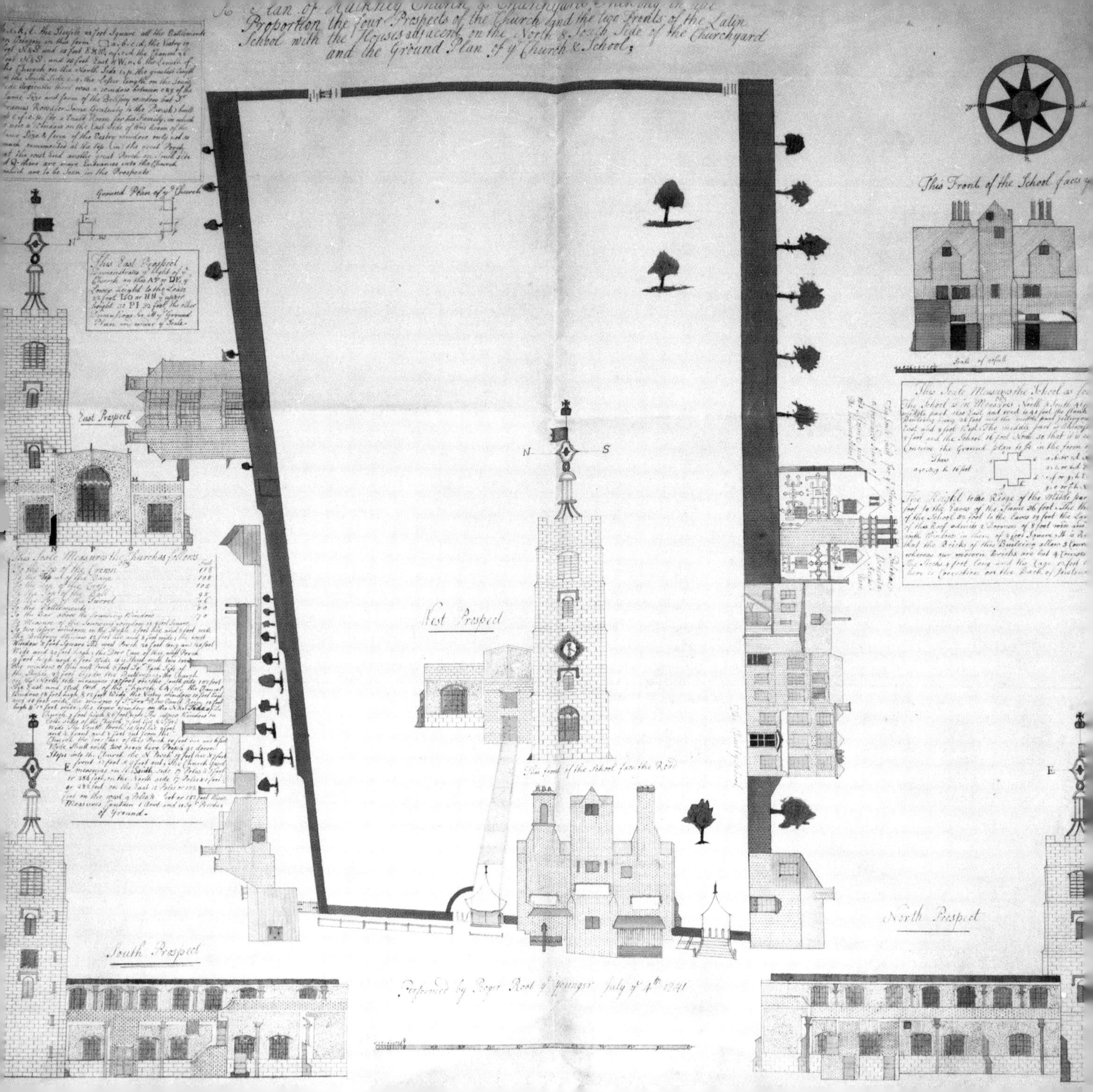
Proportion the four Prospects of the Church and the two Fronts of the Latin
School with the Houses adjacent on the North & South Side of the Churchyard
and the Ground Plan of ye Church & School.
Ground Plan of ye Church
East Prospect
N
S
West Prospect
This front of the School face the Road
South Prospect
North Prospect
Performed by Roger Root ye younger July ye 4th 1741

Hackney: 1612

Margaret Willes

Today, the predominant colour in Hackney is grey – buildings and streets. But a visitor in 1612 would have seen a landscape principally of green – fields, some woods, with little settlements strung out along roads and tracks – and here and there flashes of water.

The current borough takes in three medieval parishes: St Augustine's, Hackney; St Mary's, Stoke Newington; and St Leonard's, Shoreditch. The church of St Augustine, renamed as St John's in 1660, was demolished in the late 18th century, although the tower remains, the oldest building in Hackney. St Leonard's was also demolished in the 18th century, and a new church built on the site in Shoreditch High Street. The brick Tudor church of St Mary in Stoke Newington has survived, across the road from its Victorian successor. In 1612 all three parishes were part of the bishop of London's great manor of Stepney, administered by the dean and chapter of St Paul's Cathedral.

The village of Hackney was situated two miles from the bar of London at Bishopsgate, with access into the City by way of the Roman road from Lincoln, Ermine Street (now Kingsland Road) and a second from Cambridge (now Mare Street). Tracks led eastwards to the River Lea, and in the early 17th century these two systems of communication were important factors in defining the character of Hackney and the surrounding hamlets of Dalston, Shacklewell, Stamford Hill, Clapton, Homerton and Hackney Wick.

At the centre of the village of Hackney stood St Augustine's Church, which is thought to have been founded in the 13th century by the military Knights Templar as they followed the rule of St Augustine of Hippo. The church was substantially rebuilt *c.*1519 at the expense of two leading members of the Tudor administration, Christopher Urswick and Sir John Heron. The church, of Kentish ragstone, was laid out as a nave with north and south aisles, and a north porch. The tower's survival is due to the fact that the steeple of the 18th-century replacement was not at first trusted to carry the weight of the bells. Also surviving are some of the Tudor and Jacobean monuments, including that of Urswick, which were moved into the new church of St John.

In 1612 Hackney, with its surrounding settlements, was comparatively populous. Church rates in 1605

Plan of Hackney churchyard and the surrounding buildings. Although this was drawn by the surveyor Robert Root in 1741, it provides a good picture of Hackney village in 1612 with the church of St Augustine's and Church House, the home of Christopher Urswick at the beginning of the 16th century. (Hackney Archives) reveal nearly 200 landholders, plus 29 'non doms'. The area around the church, known as Church Street, had 34 rate payers, but the most prosperous part of the parish was nearby Homerton with 49 contributors. Several were aristocrats, while others were City merchants. Hackney could offer a healthy environment – one Tudor courtier remarked about how the village was not affected by the plague – yet was within easy access to London. As the 17th century progressed the proportion between aristocrat and trade was to alter, when the royal court moved westwards to St James's Palace and Whitehall, but in 1612 it was fairly evenly balanced.

To the north-west of Hackney was the parish of St Mary's in Stoke Newington, with its little church associated from the 14th century with the dean and chapter of St Paul's Cathedral. In the mid-16th century the lord of the manor and humanist scholar, William Patten, undertook an almost complete reconstruction of the building, making it a rare example of a church built in the troubled period of the Elizabethan Settlement. It served a community that was much smaller than Hackney, with approximately 80 households, although the composition of the population was very similar, with aristocrats and rich merchants alongside working men and women. Stoke Newington's position on Ermine Street meant that it supported several hostelries.

In the play, *Knight of the Burning Pestle*, written in the first years of the 17th century, Beaumont and Fletcher referred to travelling out from London 'to Hogsden [Hoxton] or to Newington where ale and cakes are plenty'.

The third parish, St Leonard's, Shoreditch, was quite different in character. As a suburb immediately outside the walls of the City of London, it supported a much larger population: the church registers for 1612 show that while Stoke Newington had 13 christenings, St Augustine recorded 45 and St Leonard 148. Shoreditch could not offer the bracing climate of Stoke Newington or Hackney and although there were some merchants and courtiers recorded as residents, they would have been very much in the minority compared to the working population. Before the Reformation this area had been dominated by religious houses, including the Augustinian priory of Holywell and the priory of St Mary Spital, but by 1612 it had taken on the character of a shanty town with poor cottages spreading through the former monastic fields and gardens. In 1589 Elizabeth I issued an act requiring new cottages to have at least four acres of land attached. This legislation was intended to restrict the growth of inferior houses that were springing up in Shoreditch, and neighbouring Stepney and Bethnal Green. More proclamations and statutes followed, first from Elizabeth, and then James I, but to no avail.

It is not known when St Leonard's Church was first built, but an 18th-century view of its east end shows a sprawling church with three aisles, lit by windows in the 15th-century Perpendicular style. People buried in the church included Will Somers, Henry

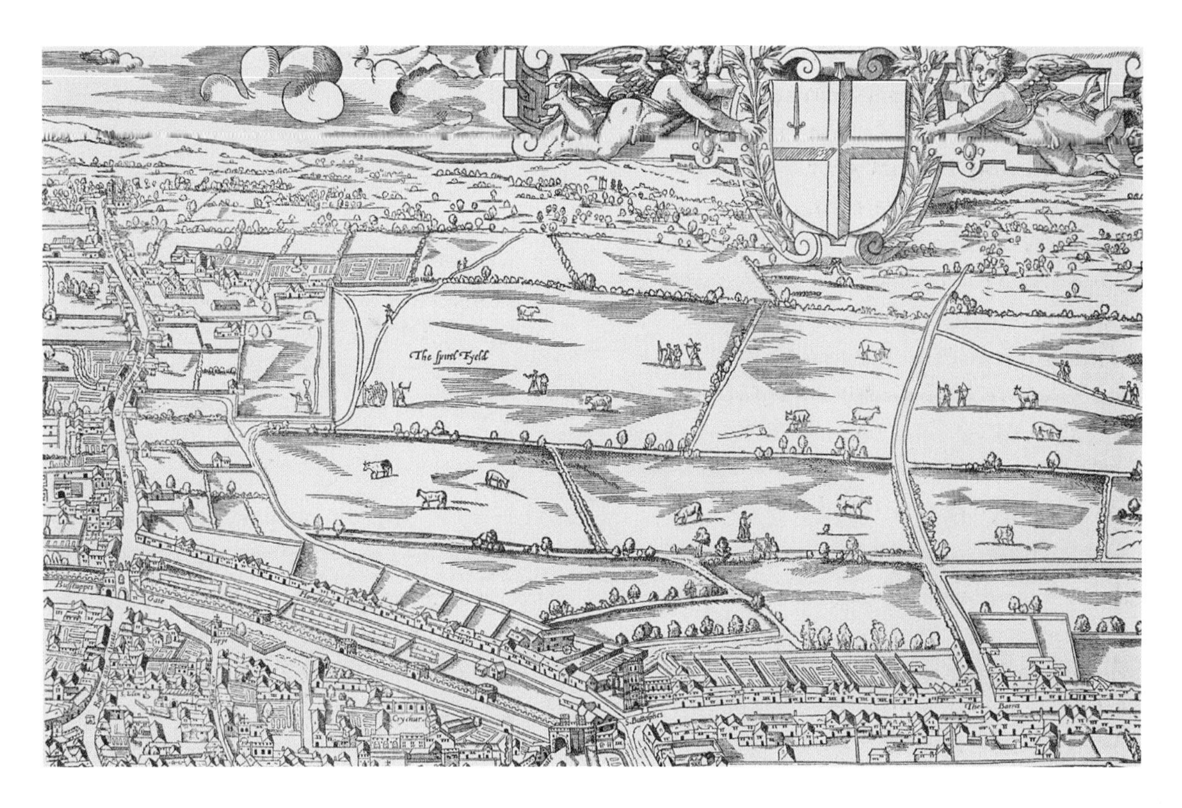

VIII's jester and the one man who could cheer him up in the last years of his reign with his increasing ill health, the actor Gabriel Spencer who was killed in a duel by the dramatist Ben Jonson in 1598, and William Shakespeare's close friend, Richard, son of James Burbage.

Spitalfields and Hoxton today are known for their resident artists: in Jacobean London the area was famous, or infamous, for its dramatists and actors. In 1576 James Burbage, taking advantage of the fact that he was beyond the reach of City censorship and taxation, built London's first purpose-built playhouse, simply called 'The Theatre', in Shoreditch, with The Curtain in Finsbury Fields following soon after. When a preacher at St Paul's Cross described The Theatre as 'the gorgeous Playing-place erected in the fields', he was not paying it a compliment, for he went on to compare it to 'the old heathenish Theatre at Rome' as the 'showpiece of all beastly and filthy matters'.

Many of Shakespeare's plays, including *Henry VI*, *The Comedy of Errors* and *Romeo and Juliet*, were

Detail from the 'Agas' map of London published *c.*1600, showing the north-east corner of the City. Men practising their archery skills can be seen in the fields beyond which stretch up through Shoreditch and Hoxton. (City of London, London Metropolitan Archives)

first performed at The Theatre and The Curtain. Such performances could be raucous affairs. An Italian visitor describes going to a play at The Curtain with the Venetian Ambassador, Foscarini: 'It is an infamous place in which no good citizen or gentleman would show his face.' Foscarini insisted on standing amongst 'the gang of porters and carters, giving as his excuse that he was hard of hearing – as if he could have understood the language anyway'. The evening ended in a near riot, after the players persuaded the Ambassador to announce the next performance, whereupon the audience, thinking he was one of England's arch enemy, the Spanish, turned on him and drove him out. In 1597 James Burbage died, and the owner of the land on which The Theatre was built, Giles Allen, refused to renew the lease because as a Puritan he strongly disapproved of playhouses. James's two sons, Richard and Cuthbert, dismantled the building under the cover of night, aided by their troupe which included Shakespeare, carried the materials across the river to Southwark, and built a new playhouse, the Globe. The Curtain, however, continued to host plays right through to the early years of the 17th century.

According to John Aubrey, William Shakespeare lived in Shoreditch when he first came to London in the late 1580s, and was thus a neighbour of Christopher Marlowe, who had lodgings in Norton Folgate. Another neighbour was Robert Greene, who is now best known for his attack on Shakespeare in a tract entitled *Greenes Groatsworth-Worth of Witte*, published in 1592, in which he described him as 'an upstart Crow, beautified with our feathers'. Greene was very proud of the fact that he had attended both Oxford and Cambridge, while Shakespeare was a country boy with no such connections. By this time Greene had abandoned his wife and children, residing with his prostitute mistress in Holywell Street, now Shoreditch High Street, and earning a precarious living by his hack writing. Not long after his outburst against Shakespeare, he died at the age of 34, either of a surfeit of Rhenish wine and pickled herring or, more prosaically, of the plague.

Away from the raffish perils of Shoreditch life, the aristocrats living in Hackney and Stoke Newington had large, rambling houses with extensive gardens. The grandest was King's Place in Clapton, a 15th-century quadrangular house in the style still to be seen in some Oxford and Cambridge colleges. In the 1530s it was occupied by Henry Percy, Earl of Northumberland, who had been Anne Boleyn's sweetheart before she captured the attention of Henry VIII. Not only did Percy lose Anne, but also fell deeply into debt, so that the house passed to the Crown, and was refurbished by Thomas Cromwell for the use of the King. In 1536, following the execution of Anne and his marriage to Jane Seymour, Henry was persuaded by his new wife to make peace with his estranged elder daughter Mary, who had not spoken to him for five years. After Mary signed articles declaring she had been born illegitimate, the King rode out to King's Place where the family reconciliation took place. In the years that followed a whole series of courtiers were to live here, including Edward de Vere, 17th Earl of Oxford, who died in the house in 1604 and is probably buried in Hackney churchyard. Echoing Robert Greene's sneer about William Shakespeare's lack of education, a body of people firmly believe that de Vere was really the author of his plays.

Among the buildings clustering around the churchyard in 1612 was Church House, probably built a hundred years earlier by Christopher Urswick, adviser to Henry VII, Lord High Almoner, Dean of Windsor and Rector of Hackney (see illustration on p.28). Unusually Urswick chose to reside in Hackney rather than regard it as a sinecure whilst living elsewhere, playing a significant part in the life of the parish and substantially rebuilding the church. Church House stood in spacious grounds, where he entertained leading humanist scholars such as Erasmus and Sir Thomas More.

A neighbouring mansion, where the bus station now resides, was known as the Black and White House, and became the home in the 17th century

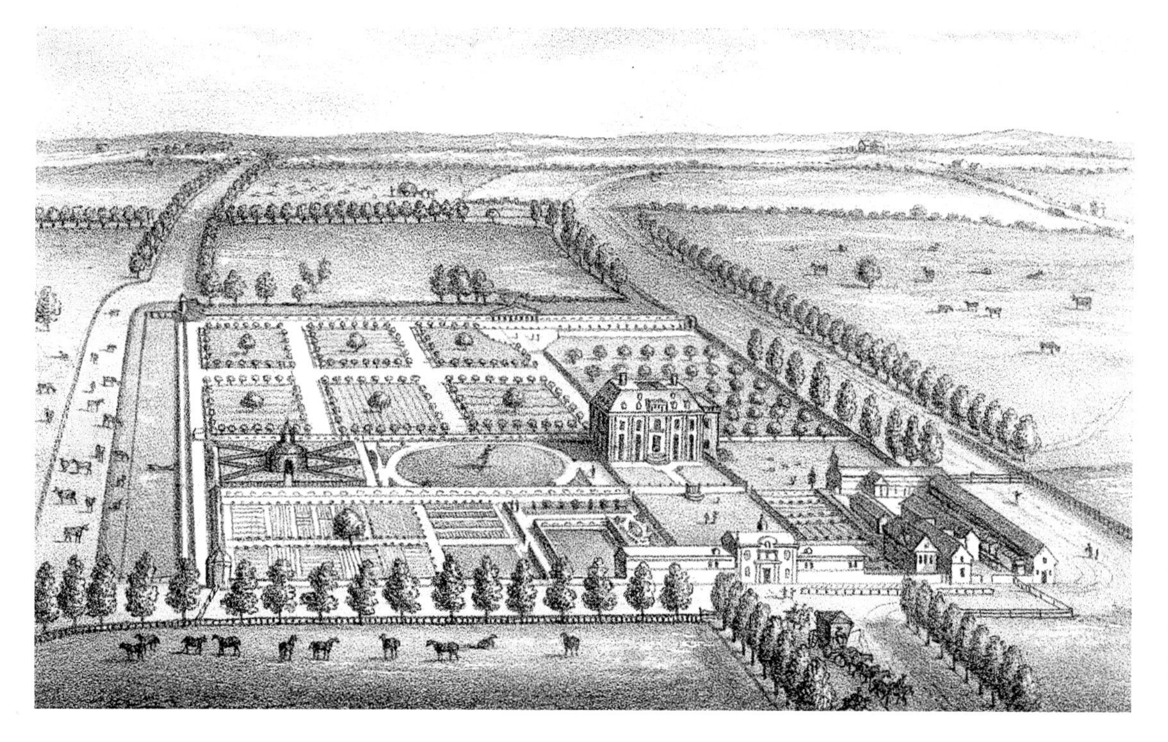

Balmes House in what is purported to be a late 16th-century view showing the elaborate layout of the gardens. (Hackney Archives)

Conjectural reconstruction of Sir Ralph Sadleir's house, Bryk Place, as it might have looked when first built in the 1530s. (Richard Bond)

of Sir Thomas Vyner, City magnate and Lord Mayor of London. To the south, where Penshurst and Lauriston roads now meet was Norris House, the home of Henry Norris, another City merchant. A drawing made by the antiquarian William Stukeley in the 18th century shows a house of fantastical design, a cross between Henry VIII's Nonesuch Palace and an Elizabethan galleried inn. An inventory describes how the gardens were laid out with formal walks of fruit trees and vines, and kitchen gardens with strawberry and asparagus beds.

In the western part of Hackney parish were two more substantial houses. In Shacklewell lived Sir John Heron, another of Henry VII's advisers who later acted as a key financial controller to Henry VIII and supervised the administration behind the elaborate pageant of the Field of the Cloth of Gold. His son was to marry Cicely Heron, second daughter of Sir Thomas More, before suffering the same fate as his father-in-law on the executioner's block on Tower Green. And in the area now covered by the De Beauvoir Estate was Balmes House, built around 1540. A view of the estate, reputedly made in 1580, shows a rather inelegant mansion set amid formal gardens laid out in the fashionable style of the period.

All these substantial Tudor houses no longer exist: King's Place, or Brooke House as it later was called, was the last to be demolished, in the 1950s, having suffered bomb damage during the Second World War. There is, however, one remarkable survivor – Bryk Place, now known as Sutton House, in Homerton, built by Sir Ralph Sadleir. Born in 1507, Sadleir was placed at the age of 14 in the household of Thomas Cromwell at his City residence in Fenchurch Street. He rapidly became Cromwell's right-hand man and by 1535 was employed directly in the service of the King. While in the Fenchurch Street household he met Helen Barre, a laundress, whom he married in 1533, and two years later began to build a family home in Homerton.

This house, of brick as its name implies, is laid out in an E-shape on three storeys, with the great hall and great chamber occupying the central block, parlours and service rooms in the wings, and bedrooms on the top floor. Although the building has been much changed over the centuries, the panelling and finely carved stone fireplaces can still be seen. The last side of the 'E' is now filled by an early 20th-century addition, the Wenlock Barn, but in the 16th century the central rooms of the house would have looked out over the extensive gardens and grounds running down to Hackney Brook.

Clearly Sadleir was a consummate politician, for he survived the fall and execution of his patron, Thomas Cromwell, and went on to ever higher things. Living in temporary retirement under the Catholic Mary Tudor, he sat in judgement at the trial of Mary Queen of Scots in 1586, dying the following year at the ripe old age of 80. He had long ago left Hackney, building a grander mansion at Standon near Ware in Hertfordshire, and in 1550 selling Bryk Place to a wealthy wool merchant, John Machell.

This switch in ownership reflects the gradual change that was taking place in the people living in Hackney and neighbouring Stoke Newington. From being residences primarily of members of the court, the balance was beginning to tip towards City merchants.

John Machell came from Kendal in Westmorland, serving his apprenticeship in the London cloth trade: he was admitted to the Freedom of the Clothworkers' Company and in 1548 became Master. Machell was about to become Lord Mayor when he died at his town house in Milk Street, and Bryk Place passed to his heirs, with the last record dating from 1605. The house then seems to have been purchased by James Deane, one of the founder members of the East India Company. This joint-stock company, granted its charter by Elizabeth I on 31 December 1600, was originally formed to pursue trade with the East Indies, although later most of its activity was centred on the Indian sub-continent and China. The Company's first premises were in the mansion of Sir William Craven in Leadenhall Street, a direct and easy journey down from Hackney to the City. It is little wonder, then, that not only Deane but many other East India merchants chose to have their 'out of town' houses here: at least four of the members named in the charter of incorporation lived in Homerton, with others elsewhere in Hackney.

The records for Bryk Place in the early years of the 17th century are very complex and present an incomplete picture of who actually was resident. However, by the 1620s the house was occupied by Captain John Milward, a silk merchant who had acted as 'adventurer' or shareholder in the East India Company's third voyage in 1607.

During his residency of the house, Milward made some very interesting changes to the decoration of Bryk Place that reflect the taste for conspicuous consumption which gripped the mercantile community as they traded with the East in silks and cottons, porcelain, and by the mid-century, in coffee and tea. Ornate strapwork paintings featuring cherubs, griffins and the Milward coat of arms were applied to some of the walls, echoing the elaborate interior decoration of great Jacobean country houses such as Knole and Hatfield House, and Charlton House in south London. Stone fireplaces were painted and gilded to look like marble, and the linenfold panelling was coloured corn yellow against a field of emerald green, with frames of red and gold. The effect of all this may strike us as garish, but it must be remembered that most of the entertaining taking place in Tudor and Jacobean houses was by candlelight, when all colours would be muted.

The interior furnishings of the houses of these rich residents of Hackney were complemented by their elaborate costumes. In 1601 an inventory was drawn up of the contents of the rectory house in Hackney after John Daniell was obliged to surrender his home in lieu of a heavy fine. Daniell's wife had been a servant to the Countess of Essex, and obtained compromising letters intended to be used for blackmail. Among Jane Daniell's possessions were crimson and scarlet satin petticoats, taffeta and Holland waistcoats, a gown of 'tufted taffeta … wrought in stars colour blacke', and a variety of stomachers with decoration in gold and black silk. Accessories included cambric handkerchiefs with laid work of gold and silver, a pair of gloves decorated in gold and silver arras (woven) work, a comb of cypress wood and a pair of coral bracelets.

In 1612, across the road from Bryk Place was the residence of another aristocrat, Edward, Lord Zouche. At the age of 13 in 1569, he inherited his family's extensive estates in Northamptonshire, and became a ward of Elizabeth I's principal Secretary of State, Sir William Cecil. Encouraged by Cecil, he travelled widely in Europe and for a time served as the Queen's ambassador in Constantinople. Cecil was an enthusiastic gardener, so may well have also inspired his ward to become interested in plants. Sitting well on a horse, being adept with a sword, composing a verse for the beloved or turning an elegant leg on the dance floor are the usual accomplishments that we think of when observing the talents of young Elizabethan gentlemen, but contemporary records show that interests in natural science and gardening were also considered assets. One of Zouche's contemporaries, Lord Herbert of Cherbury, wrote in his autobiography: 'I conceive it is a fine study, and worthy a gentleman to be a good botanic, that so he may know the nature of all herbs and plants, being our fellow-creatures, and made for the use of man … it will not be amiss to distinguish by themselves such herbs as are in gardens, and are exotics, and are transplanted hither.'

In the 1590s Zouche created at his house in Homerton one of the most important physic gardens in England. Many apothecaries had physic gardens to cultivate the medicinal herbs for their trade, but Zouche clearly went further than this in his horticultural endeavours. At this time the distinguished Flemish botanist Clusius was establishing the botanical garden attached to the Dutch university in Leiden, where a third of the plants were strictly of medicinal interest while the rest were exotics and ornamentals, and Zouche's garden would seem to have followed this model.

Reconstruction of linenfold panelling in Bryk Place, showing the brilliant colours that were used to decorate Tudor and Jacobean interiors. (Richard Bond)

Matthias L'Obel, the supervisor of Lord Zouche's garden in Homerton. This drawing is based on his image in an early 17th-century herbal. (Wellcome Library, London)

From the few references that we have, we know that it included exotic plants from the Ottoman Empire such as *Hyacinthus stellaris Bizantinus,* the starry Byzantine hyacinth. Around the year 1592 he appointed another distinguished Flemish botanist, Matthias L'Obel, after whom the lobelia is named, as superintendent of the garden. L'Obel travelled with Zouche on an ambassadorial visit to the king of Denmark, taking the opportunity to bring back new varieties of plants, some of which are recorded in the famous herbal of John Gerard, published in 1597. The garden clearly contained orchards, for another gardening writer commended Zouche on his skill in transplanting mature fruit trees such as apples and damsons.

As Zouche's garden proves, the soil of Hackney and Stoke Newington was excellent for horticulture. In the mid-1590s, a series of disastrous harvests caused by unceasing rain and tempestuous winds had rotted the corn, not only in England, but throughout Europe, so that it was said that the poor in Germany and Italy resorted to whatever was edible, including cats, dogs and even snakes. In London this dearth is reflected in the burial records of some parishes, showing a marked rise in deaths, probably from malnutrition. The City's population, moreover, had grown sharply through the previous decades, from 70,000 in 1550 to 200,000 by 1600. The pressure on land within the City walls meant that many inhabitants no longer had gardens and were thus very dependent on imported food. *A Midsummer Night's Dream* was written at this period, and Shakespeare was probably making reference to these malign visitations when he has Titania describing the effects of her quarrel with Oberon:

The fold stands empty in the drowned field,
And crows are fatted with the murrion flock;
The nine men's morris is fill'd up with mud,
And the quaint mazes in the wanton green
For lack of tread are undistinguishable

The games played by villagers, such as nine men's morris, may have been drowned out, but for the working men and women of Hackney, this disaster offered an opportunity. From the 1570s Protestant refugees from religious persecution in Europe had been settling in England, particularly in the East Anglian ports and in Sandwich in Kent, bringing with them their skill in market gardening, and now this skill proved vital. By the early 17th century, market gardens were being created in a ring round London, from Battersea and Fulham on the west to Hackney on the east. While Fulham was famous for its carrots, Hackney was renowned for small, sweet turnips. In his herbal John Gerard described how the village women took the vegetables to be sold at the market cross in Cheapside. One firm advocate of root vegetables was Hugh Platt, son of a rich London brewer, who thus had the money to devote his time to writing. In a treatise written in 1596 in the midst of the dearth he explored various substitutes for conventional bread flours and also suggested alternatives such as cakes made of parsnip meal.

The market gardeners not only came to the rescue of beleaguered London in the 1590s, but also brought about a revolution in eating habits. Courtiers such as Sir Ralph Sadleir would have eaten meat and fish dressed with rich sauces, followed by dishes of sweetmeats. Vegetables were the diet of the poor, and root vegetables were particularly despised as farmers would feed their cattle with turnips. William Forrest, writing in 1548 neatly summed up this attitude: 'Our English nature cannot live by roots. By waters, herbs, or such beggary baggage. That may well serve for vile outlandish coats.' By the late 16th century, however, new vegetables such as artichokes and asparagus began to feature in the diet of the wealthy. Even the turnip was no longer dismissed. John Parkinson wrote in 1629 of how they were 'often seene as a dish at good mens tables'. Fruit had traditionally been eaten cooked. Sir Thomas Elyot in his book on diet, *Castel of Helth*, published in 1541, warned 'Fruites generally are noyfulle to man and do ingender ill humours.' The one exception he made was peaches, which he advised 'do less harme and do make better juice in the body, for they are not too soone corrupted being eaten'. The dangers were thought to be greatest when epidemics hit London, and the sale of raw fruit in the streets was forbidden during the plague of 1569, so that households were advised to bake orchard fruit like apples and pears for a long time in pies. By the end of the century fruit had become desirable, and a lease was recorded for an orchard in Stoke Newington in 1597 to a London fruiterer for the cultivation of apples, pears, cherries, plums, medlars, filbert and barberries.

The village women described by John Gerard would have taken their fruit and vegetables to market in the City of London in baskets on their backs. One of their routes was along Sylvester Path, an ancient pedestrian way that crosses Wilton Way and continues southwards over what is now the square in front of the Town Hall. Across Reading Lane its name changes to Hackney Grove and Martello Street, where it leads into London Fields and beyond. So important was it to maintain the route that Margaret Audley, widow of a London skinner, left the considerable sum of £700 to her husband's livery company at her death in 1617. This included £4 per annum for the repair of bridges, stiles, and rails made at her own cost between Clapton, Hackney and Shoreditch. Sixteen years later David Doulben, Bishop of Bangor, and former vicar of Hackney, left £30 'to the poorest sort of people maintaining their livelihood by carriage of burthens to the City of London … for continuing and repairing the causeway or footway leading from Clapton and Hackney church into Shoreditch.'

The monument to David Doulben, Bishop of Bangor and generous benefactor to the residents of Hackney. It is now in the Urswick Chapel of St John at Hackney Church. (www.hayleymadden.com)

Meat for the London market was another important part of Hackney's economy in 1612. Local farmers provided animals for the City butchers, while drovers brought their animals from further afield to the London markets. Poultry from Suffolk, cows and sheep from Essex, crossed the River Lea, gathering in the Millfields in Clapton. For most of the Middle Ages the fields had belonged first to the Knights Templar and then to the Hospitallers. By customary law, this land, along with most of Hackney Downs, Well Street Common and the marshes themselves was common or Lammas land. Lammas was an ancient feast day celebrating the first fruits of the harvest, at this period fixed as the first day of August. Once the arable crops had been harvested, then tenants of the manor could turn their beasts on to the land for winter. The journey taken by the drovers can still clearly be seen in the modern streets from Millfields down to Mare Street. Some animals were then driven onto London Fields. Here too there were grazing rights from Lammas through to Lady Day, 25 March, and the animals would be fed before their final journey into the City, to markets at Smithfield, Stocks and Leadenhall.

To keep the drovers, as opposed to their animals, fed and watered, a cluster of hostelries had been established along Mare Street by 1593, including the Nag's Head, the Horse and Groom and the Flying

Horse, with more on Broadway Market, such as the Cat and Shoulder of Mutton. Stoke Newington, slightly further west, lay by Ermine Street, and thus received the flocks coming down south from Scotland, so here too there were inns such as the Rose and Crown, the Falcon and the Three Crowns, which is supposed to have been so named because James I paused here on his way to London to take the throne in 1603. These hostelries must have been the English equivalent of the caravanserai on the Silk Road across Asia, with individuals given the role of banker among the drovers, to ensure that their money was safeguarded and accommodation paid for.

Records of the lives of ordinary men and women living in Hackney and the surrounding hamlets and villages are very sparse compared to those for the aristocrats and the merchants. However, glimpses can be caught. The most numerous references are to victuallers and vintners, not surprising considering the importance of the system of routes. Some of Hackney's soil was brick-earth, and brick-makers are often mentioned. Rather more unexpected are references to silk weavers, from 1609. These may well have been Huguenot refugees making their way from Norwich down to London, pioneers of the industry that was to make Spitalfields famous.

Hackney was very rich, its contribution to an assessment of Middlesex in 1614 was exceeded only by those of Stepney and Harrow. And the wealthy residents wanted to keep it that way. An early example of nimbyism is recorded when an unusual system of government was instituted in 1613, whereby a select vestry co-existed with a wider body of parishioners. The former slapped a temporary ban on the division of cottages or building of new ones, alarmed at the immigration of poor into the parish.

Evidence of more charitable intentions is shown by wills of the period. Sir Henry Rowe, formerly Lord Mayor of London, died in 1612, leaving £200 to the Mercers' Company for a series of gifts, including £2 12s to Hackney for twelve penny loaves to be distributed to the poor on Sundays, and £2 4s for coals. One of Margaret Audley's bequests was the annual sum of £20 for the schoolmaster of the grammar school that was probably accommodated in Church House next to St Augustine's Church.

However, even Margaret Audley's total bequest to the Skinners' Company is small in comparison with that left by Thomas Sutton. Nothing is known of his career until 1569, when he was 37, although he clearly had connections with the Dudley brothers, Ambrose, Earl of Warwick and Robert, Earl of Leicester, and with Thomas Howard, Duke of Norfolk. As the Dudleys were usually at daggers drawn with Howard, the fact that they all furthered Sutton's career shows he was a man of remarkable competence. Through their patronage he was able to acquire properties and to control coalfields in Northumberland, the richest in Europe. In 1582 he married the widow of John Dudley, a rich brewer and cousin to the Earls, and moved into her house in Stoke Newington.

From here, and a London house which he leased at Broken Wharf on the Thames, he carried on his business, the management of his lands and money lending, becoming fabulously rich. At his wife's death, Sutton moved to Homerton, buying the Tan House next to Bryk Place. In the 20th century the National Trust, when they acquired Bryk Place, called it Sutton House, thinking that somebody so rich must have lived there. In fact, Sutton was very careful with his money, living simply with few servants or visitors. When asked what he was going to do with his fortune, his only answer was that he held it in trust for the poor, and this is precisely what he did. When he died in 1612, ignoring the claims of his illegitimate son and other members of his family, he left his fortune – said to be the largest belonging to a commoner in England at that time – to found a hospital and school. These were to be housed in the Charterhouse, the dissolved Carthusian monastery in Clerkenwell. When Ben Jonson wrote his famous comedy, *Volpone*, it is thought that he based the miserly leading character on Sutton. Sutton's Charterhouse hospital and school have survived to the present day.

1612, the year of Sutton's death and the revelation of his spectacular bequest, was also the year when the Olympic Games were first held in England. James I was keen that country pastimes should not be suppressed by local Puritanism, so granted a license to found the Cotswold Olimpicks in the Vale of Evesham, near Chipping Camden to Captain Robert Dover, a lawyer enthused by sport. Dover's games were held yearly on the Thursday and Friday of Whitsun week, and probably represent a continuation of the traditional forms of Whitsun festivity.

A detailed contemporary account is to be found in the *Annalia Dubrensia*, published in London in 1636, which includes a delightful frontispiece showing Robert Dover astride his horse acting as master of ceremonies. He is presiding over all kinds of activities for all levels of society, including horse-racing, hare-coursing, wrestling, jumping, tumbling, balloon (a mixture of football and handball), throwing the sledge hammer and pike exercises. At the top of the illustration is 'Dover's Castle', which was built out of boards so that it could be stored away when the games were over. It is armed with light guns that could be fired from time to time: a cross between a public address system and a starting gun.

The book also provides 33 poems by poets including Michael Drayton. In 1612 Drayton published the first part of his extraordinary poem, *Poly-Olbion*, in praise of the glories and beauties of England, in which he included Dover and his Olimpicks. He also made clear in his contributory poem that these 'Brave Annual Assemblies' were derived from the classical Greek games, and included not only physical sports but cultural activities too, such as a chess tournament, virgins dancing and singing competitions. William Denny in his poem described the last two events:

Tripping Nymphs doe skip about the Hills,
And in Meanders twine vale-crowning rills,
While shepherdesses sing sweet Roundelays,
In honour of the Sport and thought of praise

Dover's Olimpick Games were banned by the Puritans during the Commonwealth period but brought back at the Restoration of Charles II and continued on an annual basis until 1853 when concerns about drunken and rowdy behaviour came to the notice of the authorities and the land was enclosed. The site is now looked after by the National Trust and the games have been recently revived, taking place on the Friday following the spring bank holiday.

Although these games took place in Gloucestershire they give us some idea of how the denizens of Hackney, high and low, might have spent their leisure time. Young men practised their archery skills at the butts in Haggerston, as shown on the Agas map on p. 11. Records do make clear, however, that the villagers also indulged in far more violent sports. The area now covered by Victoria Park and its surrounds was a wood owned by the bishop of London. Londoners resisted attempts by the bishops to enclose it for private hunting parties, and claimed that from time immemorial citizens had the right to hunt here for hares, foxes, rabbits and 'other beasts'. Bird shooting, and coursing for rabbit and hare, also took place on Hackney Marshes. Sadly there are no records of tripping nymphs and singing shepherdesses in Jacobean Hackney.

The frontispiece of Robert Dover's *Annalia Dubrensia,* showing the Olimpick Games that were first held in 1612. (British Library)

Hackney: 1712

Matthew Green

By the dawn of the 18th century, Hackney had become the playground of the middle classes. With their gated residences, gleaming carriages and pristine bowling greens, the villages and hamlets of Hackney now housed not Renaissance courtiers but aspirational citizens who had risen to wealth through trade and finance.

'The greatest ambition of the London shopkeeper', according to Dr Johnson, 'is to retire to Stratford or Hackney.' For Daniel Defoe, writing in 1722, Hackney was 'so remarkable for the retreat of wealthy citizens'. He never ceased to be amazed by the number of conveyances parked in driveways, wryly suggesting that the villages contained more coaches than Christians.

With the partial exception of Hoxton and Shoreditch, the Hackney villages and hamlets – identified by Defoe as Hackney, Homerton, Clapton, Hackney Wick, Shacklewell, Dalston, Kingsland, Cambridge Heath and Newington – were leisurely, bucolic retreats for the genteel classes. Some commuted into the City of London each day; others were retired. These people worked hard and played hard. They were passionate about their leisure pursuits, taking their bathing, shuffle-boarding, cherry-eating, gardening, coffee-drinking, fishing, horse-racing and horse-swimming very seriously indeed. Truly, this was a *bourgeois* paradise.

Although Hackney and Stoke Newington had reasonably large populations in the 18th century, they were still recognisably rural. Hackney, Dalston, Shacklewell, Homerton and Clapton contained a total of 3,300 people in 1765; a string of exclusive commuter villages in tone if not in size, comparable to somewhere like Henley-on-Thames or Gerard's Cross today.

But although Hackney may have seemed the height of respectability, beneath its picture-postcard surface lurked deadly whirlpools of danger, depravity and madness. A journey made from Hackney Marshes to the border with Islington and back again one hot August afternoon resulted in tragedy, as the *London Evening Post* reported:

Wednesday forenoon a wild bullock, pursued by a great number of people, ran from Hackney Marsh through Homerton, Hackney, Dalston, and Shacklewell, passing through several nurseries, gardens, and other enclosures,

One of Thomas Rowlandson's caricatures 'Views of London': a scene of chaos by the Cambridge Heath turnpike, the inhabitants of Hackney seen in all their diversity. In the distance, a carriage sets off down Hackney Road towards the City where the dome of St Paul's dominates the skyline. (British Museum Prints & Drawings) *and clearing hedges, ditches, and other fences almost with the agility of a horse trained to the chase. Having got into the bowling-green of Shacklewell Coffee-house, he was there haltered; but, soon breaking loose, he crossed over the fields to Clapton, and running through the turnpike, in the road leading to Lea Bridge, he gored an elderly woman in so terrible a manner that she died soon after.*

After ploughing down another woman and a child in Clapton, the beast was eventually shot at the foot of the Lea Bridge.

Much of what we see in Hackney today can be traced back to the 19th, 20th and 21st centuries: the Victorian terraces, warehouses, railway stations, canals, town halls and libraries, public parks, high-rise and low-rise council blocks and the Olympic Parks. But these were imprinted on an earlier landscape. Much of 18th-century Hackney is lost, ruined or forgotten. Or, like the Hackney Brook which flows underneath Mare Street, it lies hidden. But occasionally – just occasionally – you stumble across another world.

Portals into the 18th century pepper the borough. Take a walk up Mare Street with the Hackney Car Centre on your right and you'll note how, at 195 Mare Street, a nondescript block of funeral parlours, hair salons and Vietnamese supermarkets abruptly gives way to a three-storey merchant's house. Gated, grand and set back from the street, it seems too beautiful for 21st-century Mare Street. Built around 1699, it is a sole relic of a time, three hundred years ago, when the street was a promenade of wealth, lined by residences of gentlemen, merchants and wealthy shopkeepers.

The mansion at 195 Mare Street, currently known as the New Lansdowne Club, is a elegiac wreck of its former self, with boarded-up windows, a filthy porch and a garden overgrown with weeds. Nonetheless, when gazing at a lone building like this, one doesn't have to be a psycho-geographer to hear echoes from the 18th century: hooves on cobbled streets; shop signs creaking in the wind; the gentle collision of bowls; schoolgirls laughing; church bells chiming; hushed talk of dividends; the clinking of glasses; the howling of lunatics … .

* * *

Samuel Pepys was seduced by the bucolic charm of Hackney, declaring in his diary in 1666 that he 'grew more and more in love' with the village every day – its reputation for fresh, clean air a prime attraction when plague ravaged the metropolis. He lived in Seething Lane near the Tower of London, a densely populated part of the City. Most days he had to brave the filthy, crowded streets to go to work in Westminster.

Pepys portrays Hackney as a garden of Eden away from the claustrophobic, disease-ridden metropolis. Overwhelmed by the temptations and anxieties of inner-city life, he and his wife liked to hail a coach, sit back and ride north-east to Hackney, the air in their face as they zoomed through the green fields of Whitechapel and Bethnal Green. 'There light and played a shuffle-board, ate cream and good cherries. And so with good refreshment home', he recalled after a midsummer trip to Hackney in 1664 on a 'warm and pleasant' day.

His tavern of choice was the Mermaid, on the site now occupied by Mermaid Fabrics on the Narrow Way. The Mermaid was much more than a tavern – it had its own bowling green and gardens, and in the early 18th century, for instance, an actor was ensconced in the latter, performing extraordinary feats on horseback. But the tavern hosted more serious business as well. Each year the freeholders of Middlesex would assemble to discuss politics and draw up petitions and addresses to the Crown. And it was a favourite site for land auctions, with fields in Clapton and mansions in Hackney and Homerton being bid for and won in the smart dining room.

Two particularly exciting things happened to Pepys on his Hackney adventures. On one occasion, he glimpsed something truly exotic: oranges growing on trees in the gardens of Brooke House off Clapton Common, a mansion once fit for a king but no longer up to scratch in Pepys's view. On another jaunt, he was inspired by the sweet sound of the organ in St John's Church and was resolved to purchase a similar instrument for his local Aldgate church to replace the one ripped out by Puritans. Amidst the ethereal psalm music, he was thunderstruck by the beauty of Abigail Vyner. She was the wife of a prominent Hackney gentleman who lived in the palatial Black and White House in Bohemia Place. Although his own wife was present, he couldn't keep his eyes off Abigail, describing her as 'a lady rich in jewels but most in beauty; almost the finest woman I saw'. His blood up, he took the opportunity to ogle the 'very pretty' young girls of one of Hackney's prestigious boarding schools. When he returned to the City that evening, he was a very happy man.

A typical merchant's house at 195 Mare Street begun by Abraham Dolins *c.*1697. Currently known as the New Lansdowne Club, after the working-men's institution it housed in the last century, like many of Hackney's 18th-century buildings, it is a miserable wreck of its former self. (City of London, London Metropolitan Archives)

Wealth, women, cream, shuffle-board, ale and orange trees – truly, Pepys had found paradise on earth. His experiences in Hackney fuelled his desire to buy a carriage of his own so he could roam there at his leisure, free from the foibles of silly coach drivers with their knack of driving him instead to Shoreditch. Inevitably, he over-indulged.' All the way home I did break abundance of wind', he confessed in July 1666. Once, he recalled peeing out of the coach at least seven times as he was driven back home towards Aldgate through Kingsland, Hackney and Mile End.

By 1712, Hackney had consolidated its reputation as a resort of leisure and respectability. There were now eight taverns in Hackney village alone: the Cock (which still operates on its original site), the Magpie, the Green Man, the Ferry, the White Hart, the Mermaid, the Lamb and the Sun. Many drinking houses had bowling greens attached, and a Hackney diarist observed in 1715 just how seriously residents took their bowling. Venturing onto the bowling green of the Mermaid Tavern, he saw London's top bankers, lawyers and East India Company directors talking to their bowls: 'It is something of a shock to see a man of sense running after his bowl and with the greatest earnestness and seeming seriousness address himself to it, bidding it rub or run … .'

A tranquil Hackney scene from the late 18th century: on an eerily quiet day, a couple walk their dog in front of Church House with St Augustine's Tower in the distance. (British Museum Prints & Drawings)

Some of 21st-century Hackney's biggest high-rise towers stand on the sites of former bowling greens. In Hoxton, there is a Bowling Green Walk just off Pitfield Street. The name sounds so incongruous amidst the forest of warehouses and blocks of flats.

Fittingly, most Hackney villages boasted a coffee-house or two. Ever a mark of sophistication in contrast to rowdy alehouses and taverns, these were cosy, candle-lit spaces, usually approached up a flight of stairs and buzzing with news, gossip and intrigue. Well-dressed men would sit at long rectangular tables strewn with newspapers, pamphlets, prints, playing cards, sugar pots and the odd spittoon, while little boys in flowing periwigs and neck-scarves poured coffee into dishes. Fired up by black and gritty coffee and unrestrained by any kind of censorship, customers would read the news, talk to strangers and exchange ideas upon a kaleidoscope of topics. Through the rigour of debate, judgements were reached on the burning issues of the day – from politics to philosophy, gardening to grave-digging, the beauty of the Lord Mayor's daughter to the healing properties of puppy-dog water.

In the 18th century, the village of Hackney had at least two establishments – Field's and the Hackney Coffee-house – as did Stoke Newington. We know that Shacklewell had one, and Hoxton two – one on Hoxton Square itself. And no doubt there were more.

In addition to lively, convivial exchanges between customers, these coffee-houses hosted auctions, weddings, wakes and business meetings. At 3pm on 26 November 1773, the Hoxton Square coffee-house was the scene of a sale of twenty pairs of exotic pigeons.

Coffee-houses got bigger as the century progressed. The way the *London Evening Post* describes the Shacklewell coffee-house in 1793, it sounds more like a luxury hotel: 'Pleasantly situated on Shacklewell Green, a short distance from the high road to Tottenham, and within two miles of the town, the Black Queen Coffee-house is fitted up in a very neat style and commodious manner, with a Tea-room, good parlours, bowling green, and gardens planted with fruit trees, yews, limes, and poplars, and possessing every requisite accommodation for the genteel company who resort to the House.' Note there is no mention of rampaging bulls who might upset this sylvan oasis of bliss. The name is intriguing. Could the Black Queen be a reference to James I's daughter, Elizabeth Stuart, Queen of Bohemia, who once stayed in the Black and White House in the 17th century? Or could it be a reference to links between Hackney merchants and the slave trade? Most likely it is a more prosaic connection, with card games.

Advertisement for Newman's best tobacco from a retailer in Shoreditch. A merchant orders some tobacco whilst his drunken companion balances on a barrel, smoking away merrily. (British Museum Prints & Drawings)

Elsewhere, leisurely spectacles were the order of the day. In 1737 a crowd assembled to watch a swimming race between two horses. The unfortunate beasts were plunged into the water and 'doggy-paddled' across Hackney Marshes. Whether the sport will feature in the London Olympics of 2012 is yet to be decided.

Hackney residents were able to play hard because they had worked hard in the City. Since Pepys' visits in the 1660s, the population of Hackney had become bigger, richer and more politically influential. In 1712 the parish of St John could boast amongst its ranks Sir Gilbert Heathcote, the wealthiest commoner in Britain, John Gould, a director of the Bank of England, William Dawson, a director of the East India Company, and no less than three retired Lord Mayors of London. These gentlemen were the local elite. If you walked past them on Church Street or Morning Lane (formerly Money Lane), you'd be sure to doff your hat and bow – or offer your hand once the handshake came into fashion in the early 18th century.

The backbone of the population of the Hackney villages consisted of more modest merchants, lawyers, clergymen, physicians, entrepreneurs, authors, journalists and the wealthier type of tradesmen. The poor were a visible presence, but Hackney was thoroughly, thoroughly middle class.

The Tudor aristocrats had housed themselves in large houses like the misnamed Sutton House in Homerton and the diplomat Christopher Urswick's tall mansion on the west side of Church Street, where he had hosted the famous European humanist Erasmus in 1505. Some of the upper echelons of Hackney's middle classes appropriated and renovated these great mansions. To be able to claim, as Sir Thomas Vyner did, that you lived in a house where the Queen of Bohemia had once stayed, garnered considerable cachet. In 1662, he enlarged the famous Black and White House, installing stained glass windows that depicted all its famous past residents.

But in general the middle classes preferred to build their own houses. And besides, many of the crumbling Tudor mansions would have cost a fortune to repair. Instead they built residences that were elegant and symmetrical in their neo-classical design. In keeping with Hackney's bucolic spirit, these had big gardens. A real estate advertisement from a *Post Boy* published in 1712 gives a flavour of a typical Homerton property: 'FOR SALE: 2 houses with gardens and orchards, barn, stable, and 1½ acres of freehold land. To be sold at auction to the highest bidder.'

Houses were also available to let. In February 1712 the *British Mercury* advertised a 'good house to be let, with 2 rooms per floor, and large closets, with a brew-house, summerhouse, and stable'. This particular house was located near the Cat and Shoulder of Mutton tavern – now the shoulderless Cat and Mutton pub in Broadway Market.

But a large house in a Hackney village wasn't always a *bona fide* guarantee of respectability. The politician John Ward lived in a residence on Dalston Lane, replete with orchards and a large stable (horse ownership was a prerequisite for successful Hackney living in the 18th century). But all was not as it seemed. In 1727 Ward was prosecuted for forgery and pilloried in London. Whilst tomatoes and eggs were being hurled at his face, his Dalston mansion was ransacked by representatives from the South Sea Company. They were trying to recover £50,000 that Ward had helped one of their corrupt directors conceal at the time of the devastating South Sea Bubble crash five years earlier.

Looming over you, if you walk down Dalston Lane from the junction, is a gigantic, futuristic housing complex on your right and a row of crumbling

Victorian warehouses on your left. Hard to believe that in 1712 this was a winding country lane, like something to be seen in Cornwall today, leading to the sea. In the 18th century, Dalston Lane led to the small settlement of Dalston (centred upon the site of today's Cecilia Road) and through to the larger village of Hackney to the east and to the smaller settlement of Kingsland to the west. The lane was dotted with taverns and inns, and cattle roamed across it freely. But just because it was a rural contrast to its 21st-century successor doesn't mean it was free from danger. Quite the opposite.

Aside from hazards such as stampeding bulls and capsizing carriages, the 18th-century traveller had to contend with highwaymen. This was a problem anywhere, of course, but the villages of Hackney were the stomping ground of Dick Turpin, the notorious highwayman, and his sinister horse, Black Bess. In fact he was much more than a highwayman – horse-stealer, burglar, torturer and murderer could also be added to his curriculum vitae of mayhem. He lived for a while in a white house on the eastern side of Hackney Marshes, very near the River Lea.

A failed butcher, he discovered a taste for brutal crime in the 1720s. Along with his partner, the smartly-dressed crook Tom King, he targeted carriages and residences from his Hackney hideaway, with the newly uncensored press reporting every last detail of the escapades. Aside from holding up coaches on Dalston Lane, Turpin was fond of remote farms where no-one could hear you call for help. Or, in the case of one of his victims whom he quite literally grilled on a fireplace until she revealed the whereabouts of her life savings, shriek in agony. But he had a more compassionate side too. It is alleged that on one occasion he went to rob a man in Mare Street who, when accosted, burst into tears saying he only had eighteen pence. Rather than take this pathetic sum, Turpin and King flicked half a crown at him then rode off into the night. Ultimately, after a string of near-misses in London, Turpin fled

A Hackney dandy struts through Upper Clapton with a sword, cane, goose quills, and an unidentified sack. A macaroni was a dandy who affected Continental fashions. (British Museum Prints & Drawings)

to Yorkshire (where, fortuitously, there's another Dalston). He was caught and executed in 1739, surrounded by hundreds of screaming fans. He was the first real Hackney celebrity.

Most Hackney residents, of course, earned a more honest living than Dick Turpin. But why was it that the Hackney villages in particular attracted the prestigious and the wealthy? Why not Islington, Holloway or Kentish Town? Why not Brixton? It boils down to geography – not just Hackney's rural setting but also its relationship to the metropolis. From Tudor times, London was sprawling westwards beyond the old City walls towards Westminster. Shoreditch and Hoxton aside, the Hackney villages were situated far enough out of London to promote their own identities. Pepys' diary conveys that Hackney, Kingsland, Clapton and Newington felt like different zones to the chaotic built-up city. Yet at the same time their proximity to London was very much part of the appeal. This was not just for people like Pepys but also for its residents, many of whom had strong economic and family ties to the City of London.

It wasn't as though London was a foreign country; communications were excellent by the standards of the day. Stoke Newington, Dalston and Shacklewell residents could enter the City via the Kingsland Road, which followed the very straight line of Roman Ermine Street. Hackney, Homerton and Clapton residents could travel down Mare Street which intersected with 'the Road to Hackney' (now Hackney Road) leading to Shoreditch and Hoxton via Old Street. Public coach services ran several times a day from Moorfields to Hackney and Stoke Newington. They weren't especially reliable, but most residents worth their salt owned private carriages anyway, as Defoe was so fond of pointing out.

And it was perfectly possible to walk, as cattle and sheep herders had been doing since the Middle Ages, driving animals to Smithfield. A sturdy pair of boots and good horse-dodging skills were essential if one were to survive the Hackney-London walk. But many did, and lived to tell the tale.

So the geography of the Hackney villages allowed people with powerful ties to London to maintain a spirit of independence. It was simultaneously part of London but not part of London: truly, a village on the edge. Because of this, Hackney and Stoke Newington absorbed social outsiders and foreign immigrants like a sponge. To this day, it retains that capacity.

Hackney was a haven for French Protestants, Jews, religious dissenters and controversial writers. These were ostracised individuals who, with the partial exception of the writers, had made good and become prosperous. Whatever your accent or beliefs, a respectable appearance and plenteous wealth was a passport into middle-class Hackney society. If you didn't have the wealth, then you weren't accepted. In August 1736, Shoreditch was rocked by a wave of social unrest after the contractor for the new church of St Leonard's sacked a large number of English labourers and employed cheaper Irish labour instead.

An etching of Hackney's main thoroughfare, Church Street (now Mare Street), in 1731 with the tower of the parish church looming in the background. The bridge in the foreground leads over the long-since buried Hackney Brook; to this day, one can feel the ground 'dip' here. (Hackney Archives)

The mob grew to 4,000 and smashed the windows of Irish alehouses in the vicinity. Violence was only contained after the Tower Hill militia intervened.

Walking south down Mare Street, if you turn right by the Cock Pub into Sylvester Road then turn left again, you reach Sylvester Path, which can claim to be the oldest street in Hackney. Here you will find two very different early 18th-century houses facing each other.

To your right is a tall, elegant residence of four floors with sash windows and a canopy over the front door. On your left is a much lower house, the interior a maze of little panelled rooms, next door to the Old Ship Inn. Contrasting with the heaving traffic and ubiquitous sirens of Mare Street just yards away, this is a sanctuary of pure calm. The road and path are named after Dr Sylvester, a living embodiment of the spirit of 18th-century Hackney.

Expelled from France after the Revocation of the Edict of Nantes in 1685, the Sylvester family, along with many other French Huguenots, settled in Hackney. One member of the family, John Baptist Sylvester, took up medicine and risked life and limb in the Netherlands to treat wounded British soldiers. He grew so prosperous that he was able to go into property, buying in 1760 the land around almshouses for poor widows founded a century earlier by two brothers, Dr William Spurstowe, vicar of Hackney, and his brother, Alderman Henry. John Baptist developed the eastern end of the eponymous Sylvester Row (now Road), but to cement his reputation as a man of distinction and secure a steady stream of income, he decided to set up his own coffee-house emporium. He rebranded the Field's Coffee-house off Church Street as the Hackney Coffee-house and opened a giant establishment in Shacklewell in 1785. The latter was once renowned for bowling, bulls and bohea tea.

French Huguenots were outnumbered by dissenters or non-conformists – the dominant social and cultural force within the Hackney villages. Dismissive of frivolous pleasures like the theatre, wary of the pleasures of the flesh, and suspicious of the pomp and ceremony of England's official religion, they were above all hard-working individuals who interrogated their own consciences on a daily basis. When they went to bed each night, they asked themselves the same questions: How can I be more industrious tomorrow? How can I make myself richer and more God-worthy?

One might assume that their comfortable lifestyle would make them *less* not *more* God-worthy. In fact, they interpreted worldly prosperity as a sign that God was on their side, and strove to become ever richer. It was the perfect mentality for merchants, tradesmen and professionals; relative to their numbers, a high proportion of such individuals were dissenters.

Nevertheless they did not have an easy ride. In 1662 Charles II's Parliament passed the Act of Uniformity which compelled university fellows and clergymen to accept everything contained in the Book of Common Prayer. Those who would not conform became social pariahs. If caught worshiping in an unorthodox way they could be fined, imprisoned, or even whipped. For a while these laws were enforced rigidly, especially in London, where mercenary and decidedly un-Christian gangs made great profits from grassing on dissenters. Even after a degree of religious toleration was permitted in 1688, dissenters were still subject to legal discrimination, not to mention the wrath of tory mobs who delighted in ripping up dissenters' meeting halls and burning down their houses, as happened on a monumental scale in 1709-10.

In this climate of persecution and anxiety, many dissenters saw Hackney as a sanctuary. The northern Hackney villages were far enough out of London to allow them to maintain their collective identity and, at least in the late 17th century, to worship in secret. Yet they were close enough to continue working at their chosen profession in the City, accruing the wealth that assured them their place in heaven.

In the more liberal 18th century, the local Anglican ministers and congregations were respectful of Hackney's deep-rooted tradition of non-conformity. By and large, they promoted a liberal attitude of live and let live. It was not uncommon for Hackney youths to adopt a pick-and-mix approach to religion: listening to an Anglican service here, attending a dissenting meeting there, reading a French anti-Christian polemic there. The environment encouraged it; Hackney was a ferment of ideas.

Jews, too, were embraced by Hackney. In 1674, a jeweller called Isaac Alvares bought a house in Hackney, establishing a Jewish presence that would expand through the 18th century but which, today, is largely confined to Stamford Hill. Hackney's first synagogue was built in 1770-80 and stood in the grounds of Clapton House.

The villages produced some pioneering writers: the feminist Mary Wollstonecraft from Shacklewell Lane and, most famously, Daniel Defoe, pioneer of ironic journalism and the novel genre, not to mention his prolific activities as spy, gazetteer, fugitive and keen vegetable gardener. Some of Defoe's work was so subversive that he was constantly falling foul of England's libel laws, even when he was writing in support of government policy. The problem was that he often did this in the form of ironic impersonations of government critics – and the judicial system did not care for irony. To thwart these frequent attempts to arrest him, Defoe transformed his Stoke Newington residence into a veritable fortress. In 1712 the *Post Boy* reported a dramatic siege of his house by a legion of constables and ill-wishers who, with great difficulty, broke into Defoe's Fort Knox and carried him to Newgate.

Hackney's ability to integrate social outsiders included the Rat Man of Hackney Road who, unable to move beyond a youthful bout of unrequited love, transferred his affections to something altogether less challenging – rats. Accounts speak of his house swarming with rats, with the Rat Man feeding them at fixed times each day, teaching them tricks and dancing in their midst.

We have an eyewitness account of what it was like to live in Hackney, not in 1712 but three years later, from 1715-6, in the form of a diary. Its author was Dudley Ryder, the twenty-three-year old son of a prosperous, dissenting linen draper who worked in Cornhill. Thus he came from an archetypal Hackney family. Written in shorthand, the diary is a frank record of the author's deepest anxieties, darkest urges and fierce ambition. Ryder was a law student

View of Shoreditch High Street in the late 18th century with beggars, carriages, and the recently rebuilt church of St Leonard's in the distance. The charity school in the foreground is testament to the area's philanthropic spirit. (British Museum Prints & Drawings)

with digs at the Middle Temple but each weekend, and frequently in the week, he would return to the family home in Bohemia Place.

What immediately strikes the modern reader is the ease with which the diarist moved between Hackney and London. It wasn't unusual for him to make two journeys – on foot – between London and Hackney each day. As a student he couldn't usually afford a hackney carriage so he braved the winding country lanes and fast-flowing City thoroughfares. From his family home, he walked down Mare Street, turned right onto the 'Road to Hackney' (now Hackney Road), crossed the Kingsland Road into Hoxton, down Old Street into Moorfields towards Moorgate, where he would enter the City. Passing through Hoxton on one occasion he observed a munitions factory churning out cannon balls, a harbinger of later industrialisation.

These journeys were a time for reflection. Strolling with a friend in London Fields, he mused over the philosophy of abstract ideas, in particular whether we can really trust the visual plane to be an accurate representation of physical reality. Another journey saw him beg a stranger in London Fields to take the Turkish threat to Europe more seriously. The stranger's response is not recorded.

Contrary to his family's Presbyterian ideals, he indulged heavily in drinking and gambling with friends in the Mermaid Tavern. He was a free-thinker. He horrified his father's friends once when he tried to talk them out of their Calvinistic beliefs. He thought he spoke rather handsomely; they thought he was a precocious brat.

His weekend horse rides with friends took him west to Newington Green to take in sermons and chat up girls; further west still to Islington Wells, to swim and talk about Swedish wars; and north to Highgate where he fell in love with the daughter of a tailor, Sally Marshall, a hopeless saga of unrequited love that concluded with Dudley weeping on the streets of Bath at the travesty of 'irrational' women (by which he meant women who were not attracted to him).

But he also roamed east, taking some local girls to the Hackney Marshes just as the light was dying. There, very near the spot where the stampeding bull would set out upon its deadly journey 75 years later, the distant silhouettes of the trees and houses inspired him to talk of 'gallantry and knight-errantry'. When he suggested that the trees on the Marsh were cruel giants and the houses of Clapton and Homerton enchanted castles, the girls giggled … .

Throughout the diary, Hackney comes across as a neighbourly place largely devoid of the anonymity of London. As he made his way towards the City, he used to bump into friends on Mare Street and trade snippets of local gossip, political rumour or even news from beyond the seas. Walking into the Hackney Coffee-house in September 1715, he was recognised by William Dawson, a director of the East India Company. As he recalls: 'I began to be a little timorous and afraid but Mr Dawson, with a great deal of seeming familiarity, called me by my name and asked me whether there was any news.'

The close-knit society of Hackney might sometimes feel claustrophobic compared to the endless possibilities of the vast, bewildering metropolis. Domestic conversations in the family parlour in Bohemia Place could be grating for someone used to what he considered more edifying coffee-house discussions. Returning from London one evening, he found his mother and sister gossiping about their neighbours' way of life whilst at the same time reproaching others 'for prying into the secrets of families'. After one particularly excruciating gossip-mongering session between his mother and sister, he stormed out of the house and headed for the Hackney Coffee-house. There, he participated in what he saw as a much meatier conversation about whether the government was right to reduce the frequency of general elections.

Despite its rural, leisurely setting, the Hackney Coffee-house was a lightning rod for news from Westminster, Whitehall, Fleet Street, the Royal Exchange and Covent Garden. Each day, Hackney commuters would retrieve news from London and spread it in the evening, as they stopped on their way home for a shot of coffee to catch up with friends. Also, the three-penny post ran three times a day. Ryder frequently records hearing a rumour that he'd soaked up in a Temple coffee-house in the morning repeated that afternoon in a Hackney counterpart.

As for Dudley Ryder, he was a Hackney success story. Despite his cripplingly shy nature, his fierce ambition and rigorous study propelled him to occupy the highest legal office in the land in 1745– Lord Chief Justice.

* * *

Just half a mile from the ruins of the Roman wall, and lying in the right angle made by two ancient Roman roads (Old Street and Ermine Street), Hoxton, of all of Hackney's villages, was located closest to London. In between lay Moorfields, a principal route for coaches, cattle and dray-carts, who could turn the surface into a boggy marsh. It was also a notorious haunt of prostitutes and a cruising ground for gay men.

Ever since the Lord Mayor of London ordered a section of the wall to be pulled down towards Moorfields in 1415 so that citizens could walk out of the City more easily, the character of Hoxton was shaped by its identity as a rural suburb. Leisure facilities sprang up for Londoners who wanted to escape the confines of the filthy City: 'to rejoice their spirits with the beauty and savour of sweet flowers with the harmony of birds'. Catering to this demand, by the dawn of the 18th century Hoxton was filled with playhouses, alehouses, inns, bowling greens and coffee-houses. It was a stopover point for travellers, hence the abundance of inns and alehouses, and had a slightly seedier feel than Hackney's more northerly villages. Some of those who stopped over in Hoxton were apprentices, journeymen, sailors, prostitutes, players and highwaymen, who had travelled miles from remote corners of the country. Some had never been to London before. Many were eager to sink their teeth

His raffish youth firmly behind him, Lord Chief Justice Ryder stands in all his pomp and ceremony in 1745, the man who preyed on young ladies at twilight on Hackney Marshes now the very quintessence of decorum. (British Museum Prints & Drawings)

into the temptations of the metropolis. For some, this meant mischief.

Eighteenth-century newspapers brim with reports of crime in Hoxton and Shoreditch. Break-ins were common. On 1 July 1712, two Shoreditch residents were handed a death sentence for robbing the shop of William Warburton in Hog Lane. They'd thieved Irish linen, silver spoons and cash. Other crimes were much more imaginative. In June 1789, the readers of the *Daily Post* were titillated with details of a 'singular and daring' robbery committed by two cunning jades in Hoxton. Returning home from an evening in the Hoxton Square Coffee-house, Mr Fluey from Shoreditch was accosted by two women who threatened to sully his reputation by making it known that he had been sleeping with whores. Unless, that is, he handed them a considerable amount of money. Not taking them particularly seriously, Mr Fluey tried to wave them aside. At this, one of the women pinioned his arms back while the other drew out a large knife. What he heard next must have filled him with absolute horror: 'Castrate him, Nan'. In the end, he got off lightly. He was robbed, knocked out and hurled into a ditch. When he came round, he was relieved to find his genitals intact and in place.

As the lurid *Hackney Gazette* headline placards and chilling yellow murder notices from the police that pepper the borough testify, knife crime is still a problem. And gun crime, while decreasing at the time of writing, remains its scourge. But there's nothing new about shooting in Hoxton. Go back 330 years and you'll find, whizzing through the air, not bullets but flaming arrows in an archery competition between 3,000 archers umpired by King Charles II, no less. And look carefully at a 16th-century map of Moorfields and you see archers in Shoreditch amongst windmills, grazing cattle and women airing their laundry (see p.11). Formerly considered a civic duty that strengthened body and state (should, say, the French dare to invade), in the course of the 18th century, shooting became more fashionable as a middle and upper-class pursuit. The gun replaced the bow.

In common with the other Hackney villages, people went mad in Hoxton. Deciding who was mad or not could be a fun, communal activity. The Hoxton Square Coffee-house was renowned for its 'inquisitions of lunacy', highly anticipated events publicised on billboards, cried up and down the streets and advertised in newspapers weeks in advance. At these events, the suspected madman would be tied up, marched up the stairs and wheeled into the coffee room. Gathered inside would be a jury of coffee-drinkers, who, after extensive viewing, prodding and talking to the alleged lunatic would light up a pipe, sink a shot of coffee and vote on whether or not to issue a custodial sentence. On 17 June 1773, a certain Mr Colchester was not so lucky. Quite what he had done, or how he had gone mad, is not clear to the Hoxton historian. But it was to the coffee-house jury who unanimously certified their verdict: *insane*.

He was immediately dispatched to the nearby mad-house at Balmes House.

As the ancient manor house of Hoxton, Balmes House must have been one of the grandest mad-houses in the world. An imposing red-brick building, it stood back in a planted courtyard, walled in with heavy gates, gardens, stables, orchards, not to mention a moat (where Whitmore Road is today). In keeping with the upmarket tone, inmates – usually insane gentlemen or aristocrats – enjoyed access to a free flow of newspapers.

If the unfortunate Mr Colchester had been reading the news in July 1779, no doubt he would have been delighted to read reports that the proprietor of the Hoxton Square Coffee-house, the man who had allowed such tribunals, indeed such lunacy, to operate on his premises, had finally received a come-uppance of sorts. At midnight on 27 July, another bull went on a Hackney rampage. Storming into the garden of the coffee-house, it knocked several gentlemen from their chairs and trampled over them. The master of the house, hearing a commotion, went into the garden with a candle in his hand. For this, he was torpedoed, bored and tossed over the head of the furious beast. He was bed-bound for months.

In fact, a mad-house industry flourished in 18th-century Hackney; no-one saw anything particularly immoral about making money out of lunacy. There was a cluster of public institutions relieving the local parish vestries of insane paupers, for a fee. Hoxton in particular was full of 'public mad-houses', where conditions were abysmal. At the Hoxton House Asylum up to three mad paupers were chained to one bed at night to maximise income. Inmates were force-fed by a giant tea-pot that spouted sludge down their throat. Understandably, many an inmate resisted this and as a result their teeth were smashed.

On a brighter note, there were private, fee-paying madhouses for those lucky enough to come from wealthy families. Fittingly, Brooke House, the representative of Hackney's faded royal and aristocratic grandeur, was sold in 1758 to Dr James Munro specifically to be used as a private lunatic asylum with hefty entrance fees.

Today, the vicinity of the Old Street roundabout is one of the most polluted parts of the UK, but in the 17th and 18th centuries, Hoxton's fresh air was a prime attraction. Whenever the plague ravaged London, many instinctively headed for Hoxton. We might assume that local residents reacted with horror but this wasn't always the case. During the Great Plague of 1665, a man called Edward Smallie rescued three poor children from their disease infested house at Cripplegate and sheltered them in his own home in Hoxton. The local magistrate took a dim view of this life-saving act of charity. He ordered Mr Smallie to take the children straight back to their home in the City – effectively a death sentence. But his action proved futile: at the end of 1665, the plague scythed through Hoxton. Its legacy lives on in street

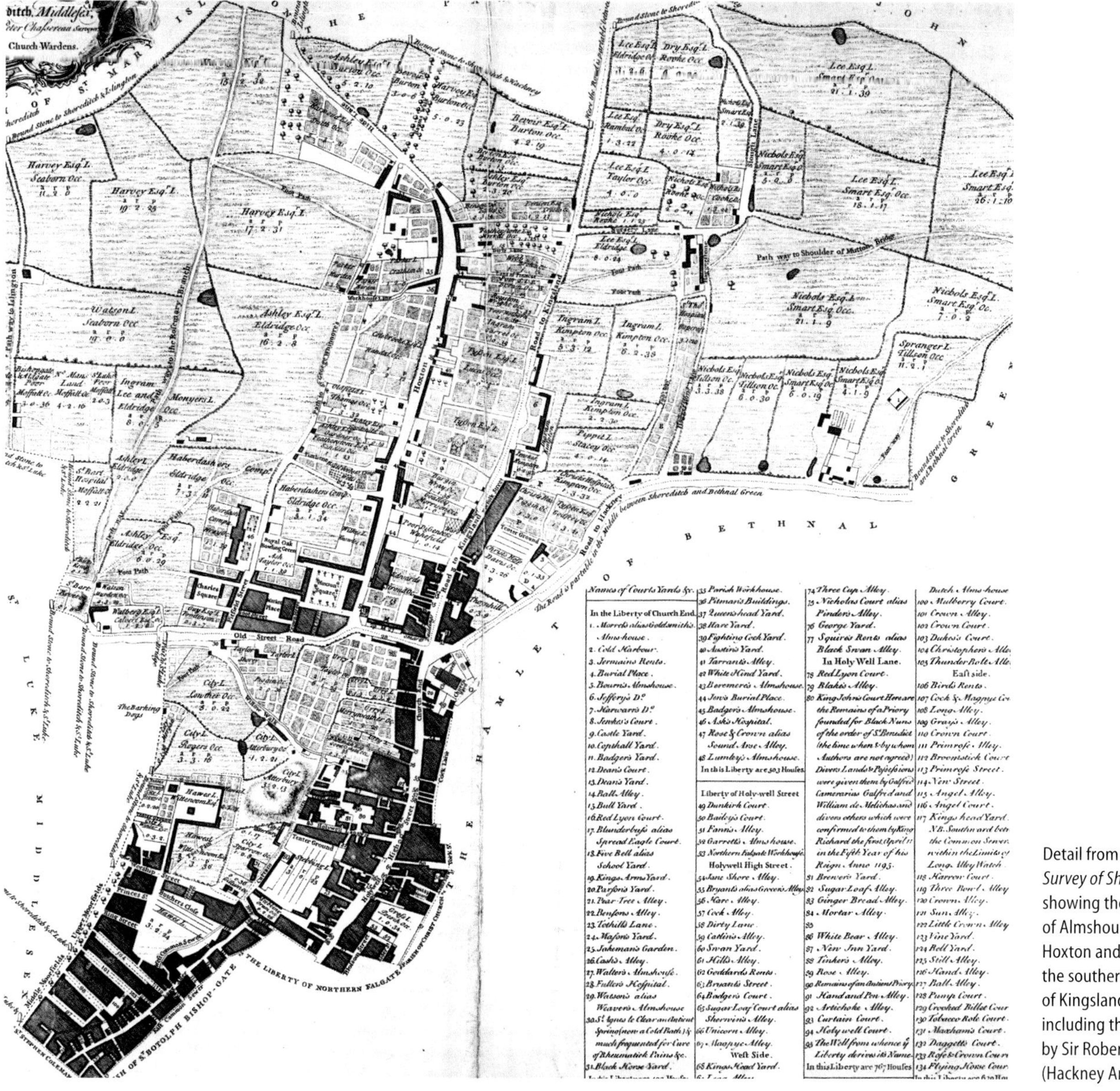

Detail from Chassereau's *Survey of Shoreditch,* showing the cluster of Almshouses in Hoxton and around the southern part of Kingsland Road, including those founded by Sir Robert Geffrye. (Hackney Archives)

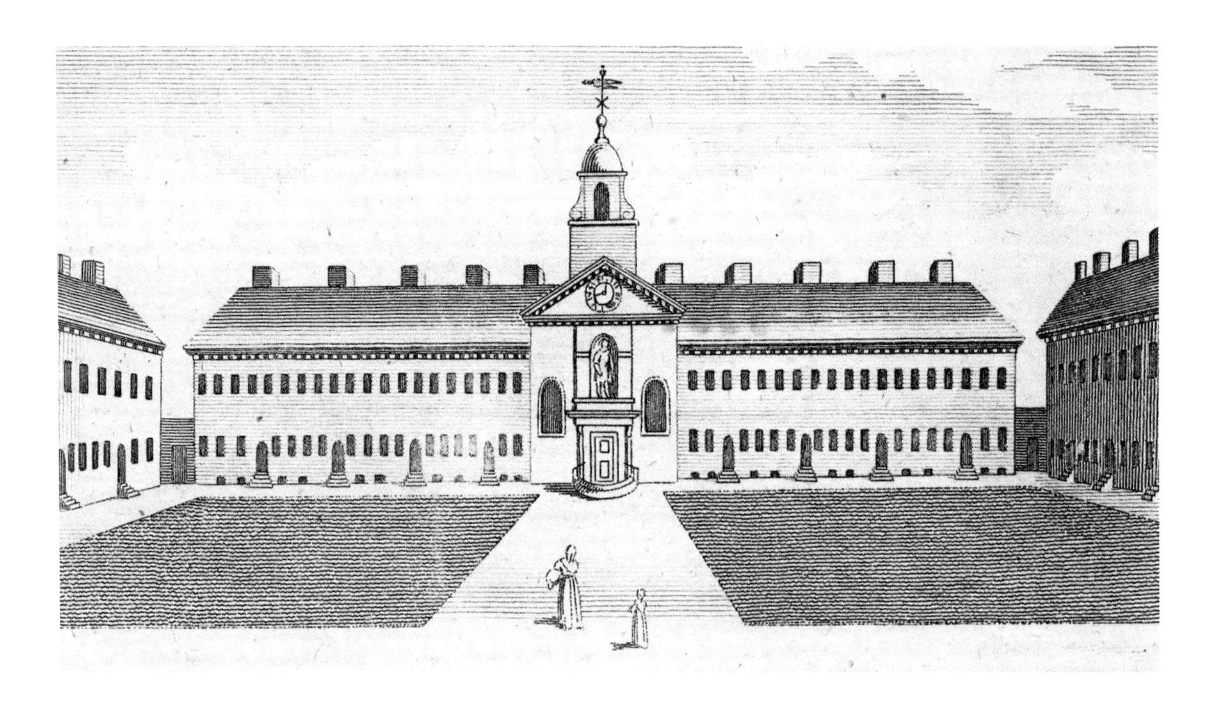

The Ironmongers' Almshouses in Hoxton, from an 18th-century engraving. Sir Robert Geffrye's buildings look very austere, without the softening effect of the trees that grace the gardens of today's Geffrye Museum. (Hackney Archives)

names. Allegedly Holywell Mount on Curtain Road takes its name from an unfortunate incident in early 1666. Driving his deadman cart through Hoxton, the driver, himself infected with the plague, dropped down dead. The horses, continuing, capsized the cart, tipping the corpses into the mud around Curtain Road. These were covered with soil, lime (to disinfect the bodies), rubbish and excrement. Hence Holywell Mount where a chapel now stands.

The urge to help the poor and needy stretched beyond Mr Smallie's doomed bid to rescue children from the plague. Since the late 16th century, it has been woven into the very fabric of the area. Even in the relatively wealthy villages of Hackney, the poor were a very visible presence and it was considered a Christian duty for the better-off to help the less fortunate. Almshouses were seen as an efficient way of providing philanthropy. These houses were charitable institutions built to shelter the more deserving of the London poor, named from 'alm', gifts of money or food. With its cheap land, healthy air and rural setting on the cusp of the City, Hoxton was considered as an ideal place to build almshouses. The first was founded in 1591 in Old Street, inspiring many City companies to open their own establishments for 'decayed members of the company'. In the 18th century, drapers, weavers, haberdashers, skinners, goldsmiths and ironmongers all built almshouses in the area. Some were tiny, such as the Spurstowe almshouses mentioned earlier, which were intended to accommodate just six poor widows; others housed a couple of hundred people. By the end of the 18th century, there were no less than twenty almshouses in the parish of Shoreditch.

A sanctuary of calm amongst the greasy spoons, snarling traffic and heaving restaurants of the Kingsland Road, resting behind ancient lime and plane trees, sits one of Hackney's most exquisite architectural gems: the building that was formerly the Geffrye Almshouse. It was built in 1714 at the bequest of Sir Robert Geffrye, a former Lord Mayor of London and Master of the Worshipful Company of Ironmongers, whose statue proudly stands atop its white porch, to house and provide for twenty-six pensioners of the company. If it seems strange that a charitable building looks so grand, we should remember that 18th-century philanthropy was motivated as much by prestige as piety – and, with his magnificent periwig, pointing gesture and sword by his side, Sir Robert does look grand on top of the white entrance porch.

One of the original almshouses has recently been restored and the interior recreated so that the visitor can see how the poor and elderly were accommodated in the late 18th century. Much of the rest of the building is home to an enchanting museum of interior and garden design that traces, in a series of rooms, the evolution of middle-class parlours from Tudor times to the present day. A typical middle class Georgian drawing room, as would have been found in Dudley Ryder's family house, for example, was simple but elegant: cushioned chairs, a small circular table, gilded paintings, sparse cream walls, a marble fireplace, a wooden floor and long, flowing curtains.

* * *

In 1722, Daniel Defoe noted how some of the 12 villages of Hackney were beginning to merge. This trend accelerated gradually throughout the rest of the century as the population grew. Between 1765 and 1801 the population of the parish of Hackney quadrupled from 3,300 to 12,730 – and that's not including Hoxton. It was the beginning of an urban splurge that would produce the cityscape characteristic of Hackney today.

If Dudley Ryder had returned to Hackney one hundred years after starting his diary in 1715, he would have seen that the idyllic rural villages he'd roamed in his youth were being gobbled up by the encroaching metropolis. He wouldn't have wanted to live in 19th-century Hackney anyway; a mansion in Epsom or Hertford would have done better. Hackney was no longer grand enough for the likes of the Ryder family – it was beginning to be colonised by bank clerks, notaries and accountants, the Pooter class who in time would replace the merchants, bankers and East India Company directors.

Hackney: 1812

Ann Robey

In 1812 the individual hamlets of Clapton, Dalston, Shacklewell, Stoke Newington, Homerton and Hoxton, which today knit seamlessly together to form what we know as Hackney, were on the cusp of change. These essentially rural communities, although located just a few miles beyond the City walls, were places where rustic country scenes could still be found. But soon they were to become absorbed into the urban sprawl that was 19th-century London – a city that William Cobbett described just a few years later in 1822 as 'nothing but a great festering sore, an infernal Wen'.

It was not that the area had earlier been isolated from the social and economic influences and power of the capital, but visually Hackney was still 'separate' and essentially rural in appearance and spirit. Elsewhere these changes had already started to happen. Both Shoreditch and Hoxton, which were closer to the City, had started to be built up in the late 17th and early 18th centuries, with speculative housing schemes such as in Hoxton and Charles Squares, begun in the 1680s. There was ribbon development along commercial streets such as Shoreditch High Street, Old Street and the western end of Hackney Road. Shoreditch was also a popular location for almshouses, often financed by the City livery companies. Chassereau's 1743 *Survey of Shoreditch* recorded 19 in that area alone. As late as 1812, Retreat Almshouses were built for 'the comfort of twelve Widows of Dissenting Ministers' by Samuel Robinson, in an early Gothic Revival style. Today the only surviving almshouses in Shoreditch are the Ironmongers' Almshouses of 1712, which now form the Geffrye Museum.

Even in the first decade of the 19th century Hackney was still regarded as 'separate' from London. In 1809 at a case at the Old Bailey, a witness stated that he had 'a house in town, and a house in Hackney'. In another case the following year, John Pittard of Church Street, now Fournier Street, in Spitalfields, explained how he escaped the city to his 'summer house in a garden' located in Hackney Road. But the 1810s can be seen as the last decade of rural life in Hackney. Other than some select development along Hackney Road, Kingsland and Lower and Upper Clapton Roads, the land beyond the village centres of Stoke Newington, Shoreditch and St John's, Hackney remained predominantly rural

Rural Hackney: a harvest scene on Hackney Downs, with St Augustine's Tower in the background. An aquatint after William Walker, 1814. (City of London, London Metropolitan Archives)

– the fields were busy with agriculture, specialist market gardening and the nursery production of trees and flowers. Most famous of all the plant nurseries of Hackney was that run by a Dutchman, Conrad Loddiges, in the late 18th century.

Although Loddiges' achieved its greatest fame from 1820 to 1840, the nursery built up an important reputation when it was based at Paradise Field on Mare Street between 1787 and 1816. This was an age of plant hunting, and voyages to Australasia, South America, South Africa and the Far East brought leafy specimens back to Britain, while reports of new exotic species regularly appeared in the nation's newspapers and periodicals.

Loddiges' of Hackney, as well as being one of the most important nurseries in the import and cultivation of such exotics, also developed a leading export role sending, among other things, tea plants to establish plantations in Madeira. By *c.*1817 Loddiges' had built the earliest steam-heated stove house to house palms, and soon after, in 1821, plans were afoot to build the largest Palm House in the world, pre-dating the famous one at Kew by 24 years. It measured 80ft long, 60ft wide and 40ft high. Of equal importance in horticultural design was Loddiges' Camellia House.

The Camellia House was designed by John Claudius Loudon, an extraordinary polymath: botanist, garden and cemetery designer, prolific author and garden magazine editor. It was one of the first buildings to employ iron-framed curvilinear glazing on a massive scale – the site measured 120ft long, 23ft wide and 18ft high. In 1816 the nursery also planted one of the very first arboretums in England. By 1820, Loddiges' greenhouses and walks were a popular and well-visited public attraction for Londoners and foreign visitors alike, and the arboretum was opened free to the public for educational benefit every Sunday. Loudon wrote: 'The arboretum looks better this season than it has ever done since it was planted .... The more lofty trees suffered from the late high winds, but not materially. We walked round the two outer spirals of this coil of trees and shrubs; viz. from *Acer* to *Quercus*. There is no garden scene about London so interesting.' The huge glass and metal buildings must have also been a spectacular sight in the 1820s and '30s, located just off Mare Street.

Elsewhere in Hackney, especially in Hoxton, Dalston and Shacklewell, there were other famous market gardens and tree nurseries, albeit on a smaller scale. John Allport's Nursery, which survived until 1825, was the last of the pioneering nurseries of Shoreditch and Hoxton. In the former detached graveyard of St Leonard's Shoreditch, now a recreation ground in Hackney Road, is the tomb of another 18th-century nurseryman, Thomas Fairchild whose nursery lay close to Shoreditch Park. He was the first gardener to understand the process of plant reproduction and to use artificial scientific hybridisation to create new species. His hybrid flower, 'Fairchild's Mule' was a cross between a sweet

William and a carnation. Aware that he might be condemned for tampering with God's work, he left at his death in 1729 the sum of £25 to St Leonard's for the preaching of an annual sermon on the 'wonderful works of God in creation'.

In 1800 Dalston was still well-known for its nurseries and market gardens. When Greenwood's map was published in 1827 it marked Grange's Nursery just north of what was to become Albion Square, and Smith's Nursery further north towards Dalston Lane.

By the year 1812, the surviving fields of Hackney were largely used for the cultivation of grass, for grazing livestock, mostly cows and sheep, or for cutting for hay. Increasingly Hackney was becoming an area of cow-keepers, producing milk for the London market. In 1798 John Middleton's *View of the Agriculture of Middlesex* stated that the London market was supplied by 8,500 cows 7,200 in Middlesex, 1,300 in Kent and Surrey. He specified where the cows were kept: Hoxton was said to have 150 cows, Hackney to have 600, while Shoreditch and Kingsland had 200 animals. During the late 18th century the farmhouse and 150 acres of the Balmes estate owned by the De Beauvoirs had been leased to members of the Rhodes family, graziers of Hackney. They were described as eminent cow-keepers by *The Gentleman's Magazine,* but from at least the first decade of the 19th century the entire estate had been dug for brick earth. Samuel Rhodes Junior and his son William Rhodes had very extensive and profitable brickworks in the area.

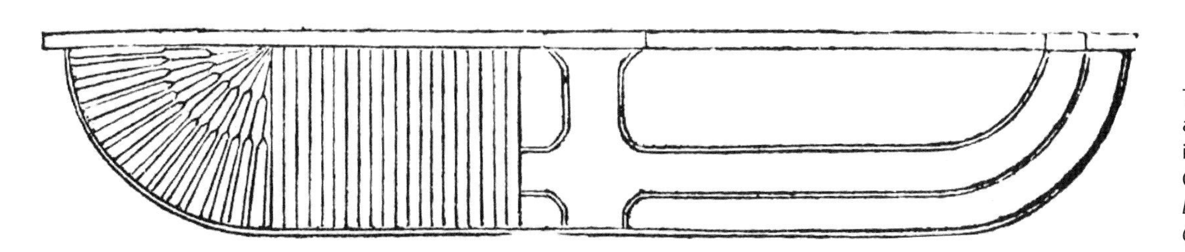

The Camellia House at Loddiges' Nursery in Hackney, from John Claudius Loudon's *Encyclopaedia of Gardening,* 1822.

Elsewhere in Hackney wheat and other grains were also grown, but arable crops had become of minor importance to the local economy. In 1812 the market porters' route still ran through Hackney. This was a traditional trading way for the transportation of produce and livestock from the fields of Essex and from the market gardens east of Mare Street, including the plentiful watercress beds that were washed by the clear Hackney Brook, to the retail markets, notably Smithfield and Leadenhall in the City. The path ran across London Fields before entering Broadway Market beside the Cat and Mutton pub. London Fields is an ancient open space and was originally 'Lammas land', on which local people until the late 19th century had a general right to graze sheep and cattle between August and April. In 1812 Lammas lands also existed on Hackney Marshes, and commons used for grazing animals survived in Clapton, Stonebridge Common, Well Street or Hackney Common, Hackney Downs and Stoke Newington.

While farming and agriculture dominated the local economy, Hackney had from the 17th century been a location where those involved with businesses in London had chosen to build homes. Daniel Defoe commented that Hackney 'is so remarkable for the retreat of wealthy citizens, that there is at this time near a hundred coaches kept in it'. Clapton was 'the' favoured residence for rich City men, and Rocque's Map of 1745 shows scattered ribbon development in Lower Clapton Road, both north and south of Clapton Pond, interspersed with a number of substantial houses with extensive grounds.

Suburbs were developing all over London. By the mid-18th century wealthy merchants and traders working in the City of London had recognised the desirability of owning a spacious new villa in villages like Blackheath, Hampstead, Highgate, Clapham or Hackney. Clapton's significant houses included the large and refined Hackney House (*c.*1727) built for Stamp Brooksbank MP, Governor of the Bank of England, but demolished *c.*1800, and the earlier Clapton House, which stood just to the north of Clapton Pond until 1881.

In the 1750s the construction of new waterworks on the River Lea and the related building of a new reservoir to the north of the natural Clapton Pond provided the district with a ready supply of quality drinking water and a watery ambiance. Just as the New River had promoted residential growth in Islington in the 17th century, so too the reservoir in Clapton promoted further house-building towards the end of the following century.

Houses or villas for the families of rich City gentleman continued to be constructed in Hackney, which was said to be just a 'trifling' distance from town. These were often built with an acre or more of land for pony paddocks, sweeping garden grounds, stables or even 'a farmyard in miniature' as found in Stoke Newington in 1812. Some have survived into the 21st century, including Clissold

House (*c.*1795) in Stoke Newington and Springfield Lodge (early 19th century) in Upper Clapton. Both are 'suburban' versions of the vast neo-classical houses that were being built in the countryside for wealthy landowners.

By 1800 merchants, lawyers and other City men were building or purchasing slightly smaller, but no less refined, properties all over Hackney, just a short carriage drive from central London. It was also accessible by regular public stage-coach, with a half-hourly service from the Bank of England in 1780. Stage-coaches ran from the Swan Inn at Clapton Common to the Flowerpot in Bishopsgate up to seven times a day in the late 18th century.

Amongst the early Hackney commuters was Benjamin Walsh, a City stockbroker who built a modern family home on a plot of land in Clapton in 1803. Walsh was known in the City of London as a dashing mercantile character, whose business activities 'sailed close to the wind'. He was involved

The elegant mansion of Clissold House, Stoke Newington, *c.*1824. (Hackney Archives)

The garden front of Pond House, Clapton, from a late 19th-century photograph album. (Hackney Archives)

in the selling of 'war insurance', a type of illegal wager whereby the insured would be paid if England and France had not made peace by some future date.

By 1800 his fortunes were high and he evidently had the resources to commission an unknown architect to build his villa in Clapton. This house became known by the mid-19th century as Pond House. Its gardens were quite remarkable: in 1809 they contained 'a fruit wall' which ran for 640ft, the full length of the premises, 'clothed with choice fruit trees in full bearing'. Other assets in the garden at the time were a melon-ground and tool and seed houses. When Walsh and his family occupied the house, 'two good milch cows' also lived on the premises, no doubt to provide milk for his children.

But Pond House was to be Walsh's home and that of his wife and numerous children (they eventually had 12) for just a very short time, as he was forced to relinquish the property in 1809 following the first of his bankruptcies. Walsh and his family continued to live elsewhere in Hackney until 1812, when his unscrupulous actions involving fraud, theft and a further bankruptcy led to his removal from the House of Commons, where he had briefly sat as an MP, exclusion from the Stock Exchange, a trial at the Old Bailey and a spell in Newgate Prison.

Charles Dickens mentions the area in *Sketches from Boz* as a favoured location for City gentlemen in the 1830s. 'If the regular city man who leaves Lloyds at five o'clock and drives home to Hackney, Clapton, Stamford Hill or elsewhere can be said to have any daily recreation beyond his dinner, it is his garden. He never does anything to it with his own hands, but he takes a great deal of delight in it notwithstanding, and if you are desirous of paying your attention to his youngest daughter, be sure to be in raptures over every flower and shrub it contains.' In 1833 there was a horticultural society at Stamford Hill with membership made up of local gentry. Within 20 years the society had gained almost 300 members who gathered for three shows each summer in the grounds of Craven Lodge, home of the vice-president, Arthur Craven, just north of Clapton Common, or at Josiah Wilson's house in Stamford Hill.

As the century progressed and technology advanced, commuting by carriage, coach, omnibus and later by train became cheaper and more reliable for Hackney residents. Fine individual villas were superseded by smaller terraced houses as the normal pattern of speculative development. These were better suited to clerks, lawyers and brokers commuting daily to the City. Terraced housing, at the time more often associated with inner London, had already started to appear in Hackney in the late 18th century. Sandford Terrace overlooking Stoke Newington Common was built in 1788, and the palace-fronted Hackney Terrace, now Nos. 20-54 Cassland Road, in 1792. Clapton Terrace, largely completed by *c.*1800, is set back behind a rectangular green space, which forms an extension to Clapton Common. Different groups of houses within the terrace date from *c.*1760 to the mid-19th century. Another terraced group, Sutton Place, was built in 1808-9. Plumber James Brown was faced with the loss of lead from the new development, as he explained at the Old Bailey: 'I live at Hackney, I lost the lead from a new building in the parish of Hackney, intended to be called Sutton Place. On the 21st of December I missed some lead from the back bow of the house, about a quarter of a hundred weight. I had seen it on the house one or two days before.' Fortunately he received it back. Another development of four homes, The Paragon, was built in 1810-13. In 1812 Brunswick Terrace was put up in Balls Pond Road and in 1825 the long, four-storied Buccleuch Terrace, with Buccleuch Cottages behind, was built on the east side of Clapton Common on high ground with sweeping views across the Lea, towards Epping Forest in the distance. These terraces pointed to the future for housing in Hackney.

In the first two decades of the 19th century the population of the parish of St John at Hackney almost doubled, from 12,730 in 1801 to 22,494 in 1821. By 1851, Hackney had 53,589 residents. Church Street in central Hackney was depicted in the 1830s as a sophisticated and genteel area, with a number of shops boasting multi-pane glass windows behind

Lithograph, 1835, of Mare Street looking north towards St Augustine's Tower with the steeple of St John at Hackney beyond. A stage-coach en route to Bishopsgate has set down its passengers by the gates of Park House. The shop marked 'Late Holmes' was a draper's. (Hackney Archives)

which a wide variety of consumer goods were displayed to attract passing clientele. The pavements were wide and clean, raised above the central roadway, and street lighting by gas was in place.

This was also a centre for cultural activities. The Hackney Literary and Philosophical Society, for example, held its first monthly meetings in 1811, hearing papers ranging from 'The Process of Tanning in England' and 'A Literary Portrait of France in the Eighteenth Century' to 'Observations on Visiting a Large Copperas Works in Northumberland' and 'An Account of the Wahabees, a Sect of Mohamadedans (translated from the French)'. There was also the Socratic Union, a non-conformist debating society that met at the Mermaid Inn in Church Street, and in 1808 began to publish its own periodical, 'The Reasoner', produced by the radical Shoreditch printer, Thomas Jonathan Wooler.

For readers there was the Hackney Institute and Subscription Library, opened in 1815 at the same time as the Hackney Reading Society. A more unusual institution was the book society run exclusively for ladies, begun in 1802. This was the idea of Anna Laetitia Barbauld, the wife of the new minister of the chapel in Newington Green, and her niece Lucy Aikin. In January the following year Lucy wrote to a friend:

And now I have mentioned our society, which is a great hobby-horse with my Aunt Barbauld and me, I must beg your congratulations on our spirit on setting up an institution into which not a single man is admitted, even to keep the accounts. I must indeed whisper into your ear that it is no very easy matter to get the ladies to suspend their dissertation on new plays and new fashions to discuss the merits of books, and that sometimes it is rather difficult for the president, treasurer, and secretary, calling all at once to order, to obtain a hearing. But our meetings are not the less amusing for this.

Such social and cultural activities appealed to the middle classes and, just as the pioneering terraces were quickly followed by suburban estates, Hackney soon welcomed the middling sort who were spilling out from central London. Brick-making and building were well under way by 1812 on part of London Fields called Nursery Field, once used to isolate and tend sick cattle. To start with, these housing developments were quite small. The architect William Ashpital, who had an old house just off Lower Clapton Road, developed Clapton Square on fields south of his house from 1816. In De Beauvoir, William Rhodes and his brother Thomas were making their fortunes from brick manufacture in the 1810s and by the 1820s they began to build speculatively on both sides of Kingsland Road.

The previously beautiful grazing fields became scarred and ruined, sometimes dug out to a depth of 18 feet. Despite the requirement to manure and return the fields to a state fit for cultivation, many landowners, including the Tyssen family, the largest in the Hackney area, reserved the ability to reclaim and build on the land.

The De Beauvoir estate, a speculative project of exceptional quality, was conceived in the late Georgian period, but built in the early years of Victoria's reign. The original complex radial plan with four squares and a central octagon was never completed, but elements of the early scheme survive, including De Beauvoir Square, axial corner sites and radiating roads from the site of the planned octagon. Although planned in 1821 by William Rhodes and his developer James Burton, at the time the most successful and prolific speculative builder in London, very little housing development occurred until the mid-1830s when Richard Benyon De Beauvoir regained control of the estate for his family.

The buildings were not designed by specific architects, but by a variety of speculative builders using published plans from pattern books. Some houses, such as those in Northchurch Terrace, were of very high quality, and many of them Italianate in style. The exception were the houses in De

Balmes House, Hoxton, seen across the Regent's Canal, in a watercolour by C.H.Matthews, *c.*1830. (Hackney Archives)

Beauvoir Square, which were built in a gabled Tudor-Jacobean style, probably by T.C.Lockner, the architect of St Peter's Church. It was the first large-scale housing development in Hackney, and the formal layout contrasts with the irregular pattern of most of the streets. The estate was aiming for a middle-class professional resident who had the foresight to move to Hackney in the early Victorian era.

One of the major catalysts in changing the character of Hackney was the building of the Regent's Canal. This was first proposed in 1802 by Thomas Horner, and the act permitting its building was passed ten years later, in 1812. Horner was the owner of a fleet of boats operating on the Grand Junction Canal that carried coal and building materials into Paddington and took away horse manure to the country. Much of the route of the new canal passed through undeveloped farm land at the edge of the built-up city. For Hackney this meant development of fields from Bow in the east to Islington in the west. The Regent's Canal Company purchased just over three acres of the Balmes Estate and in 1820 the canal was cut through the southern portion of the estate south of the 17th-century house, which by this date was used as an asylum. The Rhodes family provided many of the bricks used to build the canal and the associated locks and bridges, which opened to barges in 1821.

The engraving of Balmes House shows the canal as it was in 1830. Landowners who provided land in Hackney for the canal included Nathaniel Lee Acton and a Mr Sturt, whose names are commemorated today in the names of locks that lie on the Hackney stretch of the canal.

The majority of England's canals were built in the 18th century. Because the Regent's Canal, built between 1812 and 1820, was of a later date, it was made to a much higher standard of construction and engineering technology. The provision of twin locks along its length allowed speedier journeys. But the canal enjoyed a relatively short commercial life before being superseded first by the railways and later by the roads. The first section of the canal from Paddington to Camden was excavated from 1814 and completed by 1816, with the remainder, including the Hackney section, built between 1816 and 1820. The canal was opened on 1 August 1820 with a grand ceremony that included a gun salute at City Road Basin. Its total cost was £772,000, almost twice the original estimate, but it was an immediate success with over 120,000 tons of cargo carried during the first year of operation.

When the Regent's Canal was completed in 1820, it initially formed a watery boundary between the more industrial areas to the south where furniture-making, for example, was already well established, and the middle-class speculative estates that were emerging in central and northern Hackney. But very soon industrial premises, wharves and factories were built beside the canal. Kingsland Basin, dug out during the mid-1820s, took commerce and industry further north, deep into what was soon to become De Beauvoir Town. Originally called Shoreditch Basin, the inlet from the canal was excavated by William Rhodes. By 1830 the De Beauvoir Estate had granted 16 leases for new wharves on both sides of the basin. At first these had few built structures on them, apart from a long building on the northern boundary of Hertford Wharf and a whiting works near the canal. In the 1830s and '40s, the basin allowed for the easy import and storage of building materials when much of Dalston, De Beauvoir, Clapton and Shacklewell were built up and turned into residential estates.

As traffic on the canal increased, so too did the number of industrial premises that began to appear along the banks in Hackney. Gas plants were amongst the first occupiers of canal-side sites to take advantage of cheap transportation of the vast amounts of coal needed. The Imperial Gas Light and Coke Company took a large site in 1821, located where Haggerston Park now stands, connected to the canal by the Haggerston Basin. Another works owned by The Independent Gas Company was in situ by 1829. The coal from northern England was transported to the works where it was burnt to create gas for lighting.

As house building proceeded, space for factories adjacent to the canal to expand was restricted and enterprises manufacturing such goods as candles, rubber goods, soap and cotton that had been common in Hackney eventually moved to other areas. Instead, the canal-side sites increasingly became associated with the timber trade. The timber was largely used for building and in the burgeoning furniture trade operating in Hackney, especially in South Shoreditch. Ice was a very important commodity for the preservation of food, and as late as 1862 permission was granted to individuals to collect it from the surface of the canal to be transported to ice houses for storage.

Just a few miles away to the east on the River Lea and on the adjacent marshes, industrialisation was developing and by the 1790s Hackney Wick was the home to several large manufacturing operations including a silk mill. In 1787 Yorkshire-born Leny Smith (or Lany), a gentleman industrialist specialising in the silk trade as both a merchant and manufacturer, leased 31 acres and an old snuff mill in Hackney Wick which he converted into a silk manufactory. Located halfway between the Wick and Homerton, it included an early 19th-century property, now called Sidney House.

Leny Smith, his son Lany Deighton Smith and his brother-in-law Robert Dodgson were the country's largest producers of silk in 1811, employing over 1,200 workers. As Daniel Lysons recorded in his publication of that year, *The Environs of London,* 'These mills are conducted upon a larger scale than any in this country; two branches of the trade being here carried on; the throwing and craping of silk'. The raw silk was prepared and fitted for the loom by 'winding, cleaning, twisting and dyeing ', a job carried out at the Wick works mainly by female workers. At its peak the mill had 'two steam-engines of improved construction' moving over 30,000 spindles. The weaving of the silk was carried out by female workers at a mill in Taunton in Somerset, also owned by Leny Smith. The other process undertaken at Smith's Hackney Wick works was the manufacture of crepe, the black silk so important in mourning wear. The long-running wars with France, which prevented silk being imported, boosted the Hackney enterprise, but the end of hostilities allowed the reintroduction of cheaper foreign silk and by 1828 the mill had closed.

Elsewhere in Homerton, on Shepherds Lane, the early paint manufacturer and colour and pigment maker Lewis Berger established a new factory in a field behind his house in 1780, diverting

The factory of Berger, Lewis & Sons, at the turn of the 20th century. (Hackney Archives)

Hackney Brook through his garden to provide water. Originally named Louis Amelius Christanus Adolphus Steigenberger, he hailed from Frankfurt, and was one of the first chemists to perfect the pigment Prussian Blue and also developed a brilliant green. Berger became a premier British pigment supplier, expanding his business. By 1790 he was offering 19 dry pigment colours along with black lead, sulphur and sealing wax. He also, rather incongruously, advertised mustard, which he presumably milled at his works. In 1814 Lewis Berger died and his two sons took over the running of the Homerton factory. As well as selling by post, the company had a shop in Cheapside, where artists and printers were able to purchase their colours.

Industry was attracted to the Wick area because it was largely empty, considered remote and had a plentiful supply of clean water which was needed for many of the chemical processes. Ironically this meant that the rivers, canal and streams of the Marshes and the Wick were to become increasingly polluted after the mid-19th century, largely because of the demands of the new chemical and processing industries. These included the industrial works of Eugene Carless who in 1859 set up the first major oil refinery for the distillation and distribution of mineral oils at the Hope Chemical Works, and the Atlas Works, dating from 1863, that produced the first aniline dyes. Another factory, the Parkesine, was constructed in 1866 for Alexander Parkes, who had developed the first plastic material a few years earlier.

But for much of the early 19th century Hackney Marshes remained a wild and somewhat isolated spot. It was common land where parishioners had Lammas grazing rights, as at London Fields. The marshes formed a hunting ground for Hackney sportsmen – fishing, fowling, hare coursing and rough shooting all took place there. There were trap-shooting contests arranged on the marsh by the White House Inn. In the 17th century Isaak Walton and other great fishermen had been members of the fishery at the White House, where huge specimen fish were kept in a special pond.

This fishery was still attached to the tavern in 1810, accessible to anglers by subscription. In the 19th century the publican, George Beresford, a very keen sportsman, formed a natural history museum adjacent to the inn where all these creatures and other curiosities were displayed. Beresford was often seen wandering the lonely marshes on his grey horse.

It wasn't just Hackney Marsh that was important as a place of recreation in 1812. Many other areas nearby were important to the inhabitants of the busy capital. London was so close and accessible that in 1808 a tradesman Charles Artis, who lived in Kingsland, described how 'after I had my dinner I came to London and spent the evening'. If the residents of Hackney could so easily visit the city, then the inhabitants of London could escape to the individual hamlets of Hackney. Never truly fashionable like Bath or Epsom, Hackney's location meant that it was popular with all classes and it offered a healthy place for day trips and evening walks. It gained a reputation for its tea gardens, inns and bun houses. Entertainments were provided in a wide variety of forms within the semi-private venue of a garden and in associated buildings. The growth in real incomes amongst the middle-classes meant that many Londoners had spare cash and, more importantly, the spare time to pursue 'leisure' in its widest sense.

Hackney's tea gardens had elements of the more exotic London pleasure gardens. Tea was served by waiters to small tables in covered booths. There was space in which to walk and to keep company. But they were far more relaxed venues than pleasure gardens such as Vauxhall, with plenty of room for games and family recreation and less emphasis on fashionable dress and outward show. They were often attached to a public house with an outdoor bowling green. If a spring or spa was discovered and could be claimed to have curative powers, that was a bonus – patrons could enjoy themselves and treat their ailments at the same time.

In Hackney these out-of-town inns and tea gardens were mainly located in Shacklewell, Hackney, London Fields and Hoxton. As its name suggests Shacklewell was the site of an ancient well with therapeutic properties. In the 17th and 18th centuries a number of hostelries, including the Black Queen Coffee House and Tea Gardens, were situated near to Shacklewell Green. In the east of the parish in 1812 there were still fields between the hamlets of Well Street and Grove Street (the current Victoria Park Road and Lauriston Road). Just to the north of the park was the Three Colts Tavern and tea garden.

By 1790, the Cat and Shoulder of Mutton Public House, now on the corner of Broadway Market, stood adjacent to the Shoulder of Mutton field to the west. The open fields and public house attracted pleasure seekers from the City and the venue was renowned for a weekly entertainment where a pig's tail was greased and the clientele attempted, unsuccessfully, to swing the pig around their heads. Less cruel but equally popular were the sticky buns, ginger cakes, tea, coffee and stronger drinks on offer at other pleasure resorts. Hoxton had Pimlico Gardens on Pimlico Path, so named after the publican Ben Pimlico and his special 'nut-brown' ale. The Nags Head in Hackney Road was a meeting place for cricketers who played on London Fields. The first recorded match took place in 1802 when a team of 11 gentlemen from Clapton played a local team for a huge wager of 500 guineas. A women's cricket match at Ball's Pond was the subject of one of Thomas Rowlandson's caricatures in 1811.

Rowlandson also depicted the assembly room at the Mermaid Inn in Mare Street, perhaps the most famous of Hackney's inns with associated pleasure grounds. His caricature of 1812, entitled *Hackney Assembly: the Graces, the Graces, remember the Graces*, shows two rather ungraceful dancers being reprimanded by the master of ceremonies.

The Mermaid's extensive pleasure gardens were the site for some early balloon ascents. One of the most famous by Colonel Mark Beaufoy and James Sadler took place in 1811. James Sadler was England's best known aeronaut, while Colonel Beaufoy was an astronomer and physicist who lived at Wick House. Beaufoy had been up high before. In 1787, he took his family to Chamonix in the Alps. Here he planned to scale Mont Blanc, which had been climbed for the first time the previous year. Accompanied by ten guides and despite mountain sickness, sun blindness,

Thomas Rowlandson's caricature of a dance in the Mermaid Assembly Room, 1812. (City of London, London Metropolitan Archives)

sun burn and bitter cold, Beaufoy reached the summit, making him the first Englishman to climb Europe's highest peak.

On 29 August 1811 crowds gathered in Hackney to watch the balloon take off from the gardens of the Mermaid Inn. During the flight from Hackney to East Thorpe near Colchester in Essex, Beaufoy took scientific readings with a barometer, thermometer, electrometer, a mariner's compass, a needle compass and other instruments, and performed experiments with bottles of champagne.

The diary of his flight was published later in that year. The event was evidently a great spectacle, attracting a crowd of thousands of well-wishers.

Amongst them was someone taking advantage of the mayhem, 19-year-old Abraham Levy, who was subsequently tried at the Old Bailey for stealing a pocket book, containing an American passport owned by Thomas Bradshaw. Charles Humphrey, an officer from Bow Street, described what happened:

I was at Hackney, there were thousands of people there, Mr. Sadler went up in the balloon, I saw the prisoner there in company with a dozen more; I knew some of them; I saw them in the act of hustling a gentleman; I was close behind them watching them, I saw the prisoner take something from the gentleman's coat pocket and directly as he did that he gave them a signal to follow him, and put what he took out of the gentleman's pocket, under his coat; I laid hold of him, and directly I laid hold of him he dropped it; a gentleman close by me stooped down, picked it up, and gave it into my hand; I have had it in my possession ever since. I secured the prisoner with the assistance of a gentleman that came up who had been robbed of his watch, and asked me if I had got it.

Despite producing five witnesses that gave the prisoner good character statements, Abraham Levy was found guilty of theft and transported for life. He was one of 200 convicts that sailed on the *Marquis of Wellington* in August 1814, landing in Botany Bay in New South Wales.

As Abraham Levy found out, Hackney was a harsh place for many in 1812 and that included those deemed to be insane. The manor house of Balmes was from the mid-18th century used as a private asylum, one of many in Hackney and neighbouring Islington, occupied by 'genteel' lunatics. Variously known as Warburton's Mad House, or Warburton's House for Rich Patients, it enjoyed a decent reputation for some of its history. Warburton, for instance, provided attendants for the Royal Household during King George III's madness crisis. It was also the home for some time of the writer Charles Lamb and of his sister Mary. Charles suffered temporary mental derangement in 1795-6, while his sister killed their mother in a fit of insanity.

In 1812 a retired naval officer, John Mitford, hid away in Warburton's while working secretly for a campaign to support Princess Caroline of Brunswick, the rejected wife of the Prince Regent. Mitford contacted the press and sent letters to newspaper editors on behalf of Bridget, Viscountess Perceval who was putting forward the Princess's case.

Mitford's fraudulent stay in Warburton's Asylum provided him with the material to expose the exploitation, neglect and abuse of patients. Declaring that 'All private mad-houses are alike public evils, that should be destroyed' he published an anonymous pamphlet in 1822, *A description of the crimes and horrors in the interior of Warburton's private mad-house at Hoxton, commonly called Whitmore House*. The institution eventually closed in 1852.

The parish of Hackney dedicated to St John the Baptist from 1660 was until the early years of the 19th century the centre of Anglican worship. The growing population meant that a new and larger parish church was necessary and during the 1790s a building that could seat 2,000 was erected.

This church, built in Portland Stone with a wooden, box-like structure to which the tower was later added, was designed by James Spiller and consecrated on 15 July 1797. The medieval church was demolished except for the tower, left intact to hold the bells; it survives today as St Augustine's Tower. By 1814 the new church, known as St John at Hackney, had a new stone tower.

Permission to divide Hackney into three parishes was obtained in 1823, with St John at Hackney serving the central and northern parts of the old parish. For South Hackney a chapel dedicated to St John of Jerusalem was built. The remainder was to form the new parish of West Hackney, consisting of De Beauvoir Town, an area a little to the east of Kingsland Road, Shacklewell and land to the west of Hackney Downs, Stoke Newington Common, Stamford Hill and Upper Clapton. In 1820 Daniel Tyssen and his wife Amelia gave the Commissioners for the Building of New Churches the land on which the church of West Hackney was to be built. Lying just to the east of Stoke Newington Road, it was a long, narrow four-acre plot that stretched to Shacklewell Lane. This enabled not only the church to be built but also to include a burial ground and a rectory and garden for the 'spiritual person serving' the church. The new church was not dedicated to a particular saint, but by the later 19th century was frequently known as St James's. Designed by Sir Robert Smirke, the eminent church architect who favoured the Greek Revival style, the church cost the substantial sum of £18,000 and could accommodate 3,200 people. Half the seats were 'free' and for the use of the poor of the parish. All Commissioners' churches were built by money voted by Parliament as a result of the Church Building Act of 1818, passed to counter the dangerous effects of spreading non-conformity, by re-establishing the Church of England where it was considered necessary and desirable. With the new estates more churches were built in the 1830s and '40s, such as St Peter's in de Beauvoir and St Philip's to serve the Rhodes estate in Dalston.

Hackney had long been known for its thriving communities of non-conformist religious worshipers, or dissenters. There were chapels for Independents, Baptists, Wesleyan and Primitive Methodists, and Unitarians. In the late 1780s a Unitarian intellectual group became established in Hackney, opening the short-lived New College. Between 1786 and 1796 over 100 students were educated here including the essayist William Hazlitt. The New College was the most ambitious of the 18th-century liberal academies, with very high academic standards, and was open to students from any religious denomination. It was here in 1792 that Thomas Paine was the guest of honour at a supper soon after he published the second part of *The Rights of Man*.

Sadler and Beaufoy's ballon ascent from the Mermaid Tavern, 1811. (City of London, London Metropolitan Archives)

Newington Green Unitarian Chapel, in a pencil and sepia wash drawing, *c.*1830. (Hackney Archives)

In 1812 Robert Aspland opened the Hackney Unitarian Academy at Durham House on the Hackney Road as a seminary for training 'popular rather than learned ministers'. This enabled poorer and less academically minded men to follow their calling and to supply congregations in poorer areas with trained ministers. It trained just 12 Unitarian ministers during its six-year life.

Two members of this intellectual Unitarian circle, were Rochemont Barbauld and his wife Anna Laetitia. In 1802 they moved to Church Street, Stoke Newington. Rochemont was a French-born dissenting minister who moved from Palgrave in Suffolk to take on the pastoral duties of the chapel at Newington Green. Anna was a prominent 18th-century poet, literary critic, children's author and a famous essayist. After Rochemont Barbauld drowned himself in the New River in Stoke Newington in 1808 while suffering from depression, his wife threw herself into frantic literary activity, editing *The British Novelists* in no fewer than 50 volumes. In 1812 she published her most notorious poem, *Eighteen Hundred and Eleven,* an attack in heroic couplets on Britain's imperial ambitions. She argued that Britain was in decline while America was rising, prophesying that wealth and fame would transfer to the New World, and that Britain would become an empty ruin, a collapse that she attributed directly to Britain's participation in the Napoleonic Wars. This pessimistic view of the future was, not surprisingly, poorly received, especially as at the time Britain was at war with the young United States of America. Viciously attacked by the press, Anna Barbauld retreated from public life, never to publish again.

* * *

1812 was quite a year for the residents of Hackney. Benjamin Walsh was removed from the House of Commons and the Stock Exchange and tried at the Old Bailey. The writer Anna Barbauld experienced the wrath of the early 19th-century press and foreswore public life forever. Landowners were selling fields and gardens for brick-making and house-building, while deals were being made to sell land for the development of London's most important canal.

In Clapton and Stoke Newington cows may still have been milked, watercress grown and flowers and fruit cropped, but nascent industry had arrived in the south and east, in Shoreditch and Homerton. While Hackney Marshes remained a wild and remote place, the well-off City commuters with their private carriages had arrived. But so, too, had the regular public stage-coach, willing and able to carry those without their own transport, to work in the metropolis. Hackney was on the verge, about to turn into a suburb, with the development of mass housing for the middle classes that came to dominate the area from the mid-19th century.

BOROUCH OF HACKNEY.
NTH (21) DVN

Hackney: 1912

Lisa Rigg

By 1912 the rural landscape of Hackney had been devoured and transformed into orderly terraces of Victorian and Edwardian housing. Residents were provided with music halls, cinemas, libraries and manicured parks to frequent and enjoy. The industrialisation of Hackney had started in the 18th century and accelerated with the coming of the railways in the 1850s. Britain at this time was the world's leading economic power and nothing, or so it seemed, could stop the juggernaut of capitalist development that had been set in train by the merchants, industrialists and financiers.

The former metropolitan boroughs of Hackney, Stoke Newington and Shoreditch that make up the modern London Borough were formed in 1900 under the London Government Act passed the previous year. Until this time, they had been sub-divided into smaller areas and managed by the ecclesiastical parish vestries, but this system was deemed too complicated. The new boroughs were to have simplified boundaries and populations of between 100,000 and 400,000, governed by mayors, councillors and aldermen. In the census of 1891 the combined populations of Hackney, Shoreditch and Stoke Newington reached 370,443. Hackney had 198,606, Shoreditch 124,009 and Stoke Newington, the smallest metropolitan borough in London, 47,828 inhabitants. The diminutive size of Stoke Newington presented a problem that wasn't easy to solve, as there was 'great ill feeling between the districts of Hackney and Stoke Newington' making a merger unthinkable. Stoke Newington was required to merge with South Hornsey, to the north, in order to qualify as a metropolitan borough. This still resulted in a shortfall, but at the time it was felt that the population of Stoke Newington would increase rapidly during the 20th century. Twenty years later, in 1911, Hackney's population had swelled to 222,533 – an increase of just over 12% – whereas conversely Shoreditch's population had shrunk by approximately 10% to 111,390 due to slum clearance and a rebuilding programme. Overall the population of the three metropolitan boroughs was in the region of 384,582 – larger, in fact, than it is today.

Clapton and Stamford Hill, bounded by the River Lea and Hackney Marshes, were no longer divided up amongst the local gentry into country estates

Bayston Road, Stoke Newington, *c.*1920, showing the ordered terraces of housing. (Hackney Archives)

frequented by City folk escaping to 'sample' the fresh air and partake in country pursuits. Instead the area had become a playground for all, with rowing, cycling and promenading as the main forms of sport and relaxation. It had also become the centre for philanthropists, missionaries, evangelists, political radicals and moderate reformers to reside and contrive their social, political and religious ideas – to be tested out on their near neighbours in Hackney Wick, Hoxton and Homerton.

By the 1880s the speculative builder's work was almost done, creating an intricate patchwork of yellow and red stock brick terrace houses, with ornate Portland stone dressings in an Italianate or Gothic Revival style. With little in the way of an acquired patina, the pristine brickwork must have appeared stark and austere to its inhabitants.

This new labyrinth of streets was to be served by a dizzying array of horse-drawn, steam and later electric- and diesel-powered transport: overground and underground trains, trams, bicycles, carriages and omnibuses, all vying for supremacy on the bustling thoroughfares of Kingsland Road, Shoreditch High Street, Mare Street and Stamford Hill. In 1912 the local newspapers were full of articles and angry letters complaining about the 'motor omnibus nuisance'. In *The Times* on 8 October 1912 it was reported: 'The number of miles per annum travelled by motor-omnibuses within … Hackney is 2,202,520 … . In a day of 14 hours 7,324 mechanically propelled vehicles passed five important points, or an average of 523 per hour.' The borough engineer, Norman Scrogie, reported that the traffic 'is now fast assuming alarming proportions, necessitating constant attention to the roads over which such traffic passes'.

Victorian department stores, apothecaries, bazaars and street markets all displayed their exotic produce from far-flung places to a captive audience, divorced from their former lives working as agricultural labourers and craftspeople. This transplantation of men, women and children can be graphically seen in Abney Park Cemetery in Stoke Newington, one of the new burial grounds created to cope with London's population explosion. Gravestones and memorials record the birthplaces – South West England, Wales and the Borders, East Anglia – the place of death, always London.

From the late 18th century manufacturing became concentrated in town-based factories, undermining the viability of small-scale cottage industries in rural areas that had once provided work for men, women and children alike. Local crafts, like lace-making, pottery and furniture-making could not compete with machine-made goods and the old traditional skills started to decline. The rural woollen and linen industries of South West England and East Anglia collapsed in the face of increased competition from the northern counties of Lancashire and Yorkshire.

What had started as a slow trickle of dispossessed agricultural labourers coming to towns and cities as a result of a series of private acts of enclosure in the 18th century became a torrent in the first half of the 19th century with a series of public acts. The enclosures had created a new social system. As J. L. and Barbara Hammond put it in their classic work, *The Village Labourer*: 'The peasant with rights and status, with a share in the fortunes and government of his village, standing in rags but standing on his feet, makes way for the labourer with no corporate rights to defend, nor corporate power to invoke, no property to cherish, no ambition to pursue, bent beneath the fear of his masters and the weight of a future hope'.

London, in particular, had long acted as a magnet to those who wanted to find a new life and perhaps to make some money. Not only did they come from all over Britain, but in this age of empire, from all over the world. For middle-income workers, like clerks, lawyers and civil servants, Hackney was conveniently situated, just four miles from the Bank of England and Lloyds of London. They were accommodated in suburbs like De Beauvoir, London Fields, Victoria Park, Clapton and Stamford Hill. But for others life here was beset by misery, poverty and suffering. By the end of the 19th century, Homerton, Hackney Wick, Shoreditch and Hoxton had become overcrowded slums. In Charles Booth's *Inquiry into the Life and Labour of the People in London*, undertaken between 1886 and 1903, Hackney Wick's population was said to 'consist largely of failures who have drifted there from other districts. Dirty, shiftless, helpless and undisciplined, but not criminal'. These areas consisted of close-knit, working-class communities where daily life was centred on the warehouses and factories of the locality.

The huge disparities in wealth between the City of London and these outer fringes were marked. The Old Nichol, situated just on the border between Shoreditch, Bethnal Green and the City, was a desperate place in stark contrast to the ordered and leafy suburbs to the north.

This warren of maze-like streets and passageways, brilliantly brought to life in Sarah Wise's *The Blackest Streets: the life and death of a Victorian Slum*, were so narrow that people 'had to turn sideways and move crabwise along'. It had also become a feared place for those living outside this closed backwater, and was commonly perceived to be 'a criminal enclave … with its strange geography assisting a street robber or sneak-thief in his dash to safety'. In truth, it is hard to imagine that the people living here had the strength for such activity: 'A ragged woman crouching in a doorway started in fright as they neared her, clutched her small, equally ragged child to her breast and rose to her feet as if to defend herself.'

This is Sarah Wise's description of Ann's Place:

A two-roomed tenement that has its own weather: the walls are running with damp, and the meagre fire burning in the grate has drawn some of the moisture out of the plaster, creating a small local fog … .This is home

Hoxton Street, *c.*1910. Despite the presence of Sainsbury's, this was a poor district, with the Shoreditch workhouse in the far distance. (Hackney Archives)

to a married couple with six children. There is no bed, and when you ask them how they sleep, the wife replies, 'Oh, we sleep about the room how we can'. Walk through a hole in the wall into the second room and you'll see the husband and two adolescent sons making uppers for boots. They are so busy they don't even look up or gesture; they are haggard and hollow-cheeked.

The dwellings in the Old Nichol had been erected by speculative builders who leased the land from aristocratic owners such as the resplendently named Richard Plantagenet Campbell Temple-Nugent-Brydges-Chandos-Grenville, 3rd Duke of Buckingham and Chandos. These landowners did not care what was done with their land as long as it remained profitable. Wise continues a description of a typical slum dwelling:

Instead of using traditional mortar, the speculative builders found a cheaper lime-based substance derived from the by-products of soap-making ... This 'cement' was known as Billysweet, and quickly became infamous for never thoroughly drying out, and so leading to sagging, unstable walls .... Most of the early-1800s houses had no foundations, their floorboards being laid on to bare earth; cheap timber and half-baked bricks of ash-adulterated clay were used. Roofs were badly pitched, resulting in rotting rafters and plasterwork, with this damp from above joining the damp seeping upwards for the earth to create permanently soggy dwellings.

Perhaps due to this combination of rich and poor, living cheek by jowl, so near to the power-house of the British Empire, Hackney and its borders also became a place for men and women with reforming ideas and political and social ambition to come to cut their teeth.

A notable local politician and supporter of the Liberal government was the physician Christopher Addison, whose wife's wealth had enabled a mid-life career change from medicine to politics. He entered the political arena in order to improve the conditions of the poor, and in 1907 became the Liberal candidate for Hoxton, an impoverished ward located in Shoreditch. In the general election of January 1910, Addison won the seat and entered the House of Commons.

The Commons had always been an uncertain world, but was particularly so in the first years of the 20th century. In 1906 the Liberals, led by Henry Campbell-Bannerman, had won a landslide victory and proposed a raft of measures to improve the lot of the working classes, including a pension for every British subject over the age of 70 with an income of less than £31 10s. In 1909 the Chancellor of the Exchequer, David Lloyd George, proposed a People's Budget, which he described as a 'war budget':

Raising money to wage implacable warfare against poverty and squalidness. I cannot help hoping and believing that before this generation had passed away, we shall have advanced a great step towards that good time, when poverty, and the wretchedness and human degradation which always follows in its camp, will be as remote to the people of this country as the wolves which once infested its forests.

Although it passed the Commons, the budget was thrown out by the Lords, where a group of Conservative peers, known as the backwoodsmen, had been implacably opposed to many of the Liberal measures. Asquith, now the Liberal Prime Minster, denounced the action of the Lords as a breach of the constitution and fought two elections in 1910 on the issues of the budget and the veto powers of the Lords. Support for the Liberals had fallen rapidly away since 1906, and in order to maintain a majority, Asquith was obliged to offer home rule for Ireland in return for the support of John Redmond and the Irish Parliamentary Party.

In 1911 Dr Addison was asked by Lloyd George to assist with the passing of the National Insurance Bill, which provided insurance not only for the whole working population against loss of health and for the prevention and cure of sickness, but also against unemployment. The year after the ending of the First World War, Addison introduced his Housing and Town Planning Act, which obliged local authorities to provide new housing for rent. His controversial 'Homes fit for Heroes' programme,

Ivy Walk, Hoxton. Although much of the housing in this area was demolished with slum clearances at the beginning of the 20th century, these houses survived until the 1950s, when this photograph was taken. (Hackney Archives)

designed to provide quality houses for the working classes, initially made little impact: by July 1921 the programme had provided only 170,000 of the proposed 500,000 homes earmarked to be built in green belt land. Stalled by labour and material shortages, Addison's ambitious housing policies proved totally unrealistic, provoking a right-wing 'anti-waste' campaign and backlash. However, Addison could ultimately claim that 'an important new social principle of housing as a social service had been enacted' even if it took another decade before council house building increased to satisfactory levels. In Hackney there are only a few examples of these 'cottage estates' as most of the land had already been built upon. In 1920 the LCC planned a number of cottage homes in Cleveleys,

Gunton and Casimir Roads in Clapton. Built on former fields, these two storey terraced houses, in sets of eight with back and front gardens had little in the way of detail, but were a step up from the crowded and insanitary slums of Hoxton.

At a local level, Addison was responsible for doing much to alleviate poverty by improving education and health provision first in Hoxton, and then in 1918 in his Shoreditch constituency. The Hammond Square School in Ivy Street (now Burbage Primary School) was enlarged in 1911. The following year Hoxton Central School was built on Hoxton Street. In the *Kingsland and Hackney Gazette* it was reported that the Hoxton Central School would accommodate 195 boys and 195 girls with each department containing five classrooms and practical workrooms – fitted up with a spacious art room and a place for nature study provided over the hall. Mr Cyril S. Cobb, Chairman of the LCC Education Committee, pointed out that the Central Schools represented a new departure. They were with a view to 'giving the children a training which would be of direct assistance to them when they left school. Anything that would bring the children into closer touch with their after life was', he observed, 'extremely desirable.'

Ten years later the Shoreditch Maternity and Child Welfare Centre was opened on Kingsland Road. One of the first ante-natal and infant care out-patient centres to be provided in Britain, it was funded by Andrew Carnegie, who also enabled libraries to be built in neighbouring Hackney. The homely Neo-Georgian elevations were the work of the architect Francis Danby Smith who specialised in hospital construction.

Summing up Addison's career, his biographer Kenneth O'Magan described him as 'the most notable doctor ever to be involved in British politics' playing 'a much underestimated part, in two periods of war and reconstruction, in making Britain a welfare democracy and a more humane society'.

In South Hackney, however, politics was taken from the venerable heights of Addison's 'socialist' ideals to the disreputable lows of Horatio Bottomley's self-serving politics. The entry for Horatio Bottomley in the *Oxford Dictionary of National Biography*, labels him as journalist and swindler. Born in 1860, he was orphaned at the age of four and sent to an institution in Birmingham. The misery of his life there seems to have driven him into a world of fantasy. But he was also a man of determination, and by 1885 he had acquired a small group of magazines and journals.

In 1906, after spending many years nurturing an ambition to become a Member of Parliament, Bottomley managed to defeat the incumbent Tory MP, winning the South Hackney seat for the Liberals. His desire to be a politician was born from a mixture of vanity and business acumen. For him, politics offered influence and respectability, as well as the obvious mechanism to influence government policy, particularly in respect to the commercial world that he inhabited. 'All parties', he declared in his magazine *John Bull* in May 1906,' are organised hypocrisies.' The light-hearted opinions he shared with his constituents might have amused the public, but they did not impress his fellow Liberals, and his reputation as a fraudster made him so unwelcome at Westminster that his maiden speech was heard in chilling silence.

In February 1912 Bottomley's ambiguous financial past caught up with him. Facing demands from a number of creditors, including the Prudential Assurance Company, he admitted that his liabilities exceeded his assets by a staggering £200,000. He had previously been subject to bankruptcy claims but had managed to steer himself out of trouble. In May 1912 came the demise of Bottomley's political career. On 17 May the *Kingsland and Hackney Gazette* reported: 'the expected has happened in South Hackney, but it has happened sooner than most people expected. Our prophecy has come true; for within 24 hours Mr Bottomley has approached the Chief Liberal Whip and intimated his intention to retire.'

As the story began to break around the country Mr Bottomley was comfortably ensconced in the Great Eastern Hotel in Liverpool Street, entertaining a few friends and a reporter from the *Kingsland and Hackney Gazette*. When asked if he had any message for the electorate he replied: 'What can I say but *au revoir* and not goodbye, and that I am sorry to leave them?'

As a bankrupt he was a disgrace and could no longer remain an MP but, despite his spectacular fall from power, he displayed no remorse, telling audiences that the present 'musty, rusty, corrupt system' needed replacement by a 'business government'. Horatio, the resolute fantasist, was only temporarily crestfallen. In 1918 he entered the Commons once more as the independent MP for Hackney South, but in March 1922 he was charged at the Old Bailey with fraudulent conversion and sentenced to seven years in prison. On 26 May 1933 he died, aged 74. His obituary in the *Daily Mail* noted: 'He had magnetism, eloquence, enthusiasm, the power to convince … he might have been anything, a captain of industry, a great journalist'. In fact, if only he had stayed working at the paper that he had, aged 28, co-founded with James Sheridan back in 1888 – *The Financial Times* – things might have turned out very differently.

Following Bottomley's resignation, a by-election was called in South Hackney, and a hard campaign ensued, fought between the Unionist John C. Gibson and the Liberal Hector Morison. On 25 May a Liberal victory was announced with Morison winning a 503 majority with 5,339 votes. In the lead-up to this, crowded public meetings had been organised for the prospective candidates to let loose a 'perfect torrent of political eloquence'.

One of the contentious issues of the election was whether women should receive the vote. During the by-election in South Hackney the London Society for Women's Suffrage (LSWS) requested the views of Morison and Gibson on the subject of 'Votes for Women'. The Unionist candidate authorised the following statement to be sent by his assistant Mr Layland: 'He does not consider it politic for any candidate to express an opinion at this juncture, owing to the recent law cases on the militant portion of your organisation.' The same question was sent to Morison whose reply was similarly evasive: 'In regard to woman's suffrage, the question in my opinion is certainly not before the electors of South Hackney at the moment, and consequently I do not propose at the present time to make any definite statements in regard to it.'

On 20 May 1912, towards the end of this fierce electoral battle, a memorable public meeting took place in Hackney Wick. According to the *Hackney and Kingsland Gazette*, Suffragettes (women who used militant tactics rather than Suffragists who campaigned for constitutional reforms) had descended on Hackney Wick 'to speak from wagons and other improvised platforms'.

The militant section of the movement was the Women's Social and Political Union (WSPU), led by the charismatic mother and daughter, Emmeline and Christabel Pankhurst. The newspaper noted wryly that the attendance of the Suffragettes 'tended to still further enliven the proceedings, and has added an element of humour, if not an interest, to the already animated campaign'. In close proximity to their pitches were speakers and supporters of the National League for Opposing Woman Suffrage whose presence only added to the general disorder of the meeting. Each speaker was working to outdo their rival with the force and vehemence of their argument. The crowd, however, was in 'a hectoring mood, and accorded the ladies a reception more demonstrative than pleasant. Indeed threats of a window-smashing crusade are said to have been resorted to, though the Wickites declared that it will not be the windows that will suffer most.'

Earlier that year, the WSPU had shifted its tactics towards attacks on people, buildings and property. On 1 March, 150 Suffragettes took part in a shop-window-smashing campaign in London's West End. The WSPU, however, were unpopular with other groups who felt that enfranchisement or 'Votes for Women' should be gained through political pressure and constitutional means. One such was the LSWS who called a meeting on 26 May 1911 at Hackney Town Hall, attended by the Mayor of Hackney, Councillor W.F.Fenton-Jones, Isabel Gimingham, president of the Hackney Branch, and feminist and constitutional Suffragist grandee Mrs Henry Fawcett, *née* Millicent Garrett. At this meeting the following resolution was passed: 'That this meeting of the inhabitants of Hackney respectfully calls upon the Prime Minister to take a further step towards the establishment in all its fulness [*sic*] of representative government by giving facilities this season for the passing into law of the Women's Enfranchisement Bill, the second

Suffragettes with banners and blossoms at a rally in Victoria Park, 25 May 1913. (Corbis Images)

reading of which was carried out in the House of Commons on 5th May by a majority of nearly 3 to 1.'

Clapton in particular had become a centre of Suffragist and feminist activity. One militant Suffragette, and member of the WSPU was Myra Sadd Brown, who lived for a short period *c.*1907 at 34 Woodberry Down in Finsbury Park with her husband Ernest. Ernest Brown was a successful businessman, thus providing her with financial independence to follow her political, charitable and artistic pursuits. In Hackney, Myra served as a Poor Law Guardian and she was also a member of the North Hackney Liberal Association. In 1912, when she was arrested and imprisoned for her involvement in WSPU activities, she went on hunger strike and endured forcible feeding – a terrible and dangerous tactic that the Liberal government employed to break Suffragettes' fasting. Later, she also became associated with Sylvia Pankhurst's East London Federation of Suffragettes – which focused on recruiting working-class women to the cause. Other WSPU members in Hackney included WSPU Secretary Mrs Ellen Isabel Jones at 39 Pembury Road.

There were also a large number of women and men who opposed the Suffragist cause and they organised themselves into Anti-Suffragist groups like the National League for Opposing Woman Suffrage (NLOWS). In Hackney, the NLOWS had established an Anti-Suffrage shop in Amhurst Road with many of its Hackney members attending public debates and Suffragists' meetings in order to heckle.

Just as Dr Addison had moved into Liberal politics as a result of his wife's wealth, so another Hackney resident, Sir Albert Spicer, was able to follow a distinguished political career thanks to the very profitable paper and stationers business that he had inherited with his brothers from his father. Spicer was elected as the Liberal MP for Central Hackney in 1906 and served for the constituency until 1918. His wife had been in attendance at Hackney Town Hall on 26 May 1911 when the resolution mentioned earlier was passed by the LSWS, and Sir Albert appears also to have been a supporter of the Suffragist cause, declaring at the beginning of 1912: 'As far as regards myself, in every contest that I have fought … I have declared myself to be in favour of Woman's Suffrage … . If it is true that some women do not want the vote, they need not make use of it when it has been given to them, but we have no right to shut out any longer those who do.'

However, his ideas on Suffrage seem to have got caught up with his support for Irish Home Rule. On 7 December 1912 Spicer chaired a Home Rule demonstration at Dalston Theatre with John Redmond, the Irish Nationalist. Redmond, like other high-profile political leaders, was a target of the militant WSPU because he had voted earlier in the year against women's enfranchisement. He realised that any reform to include votes for women would have to occur alongside general election reform, including redistribution of seats, which would help to strengthen the Ulster Unionists and Sinn Féin. On 18 July Redmond was wounded when Mary Leigh, a member of the WSPU, threw a hatchet into the carriage in which he was travelling with the Prime Minister, Asquith, during a visit to Dublin.

At the meeting in Dalston Theatre a large number of stewards were deployed throughout, and a strong 'posse' of police guarded the outside of the building. Early in the proceedings it was apparent that the Suffragettes and their male supporters were also present in considerable numbers. Redmond was welcomed by a chant of 'For he's a jolly good fellow' accompanied by Irish pipers, but as he rose to speak a woman shouted: 'Why are you obstructing woman's suffrage?' She was quickly hustled out and Redmond was given an ovation.

An interior from the photograph album of the Gaviller family, *c.*1910. The Gavillers lived at 183 Lower Clapton Road, a comfortable middle-class area in the early 20th century. (Hackney Archives)

During the course of this meeting scuffles broke out: blows were exchanged in the gallery, while well-dressed ladies in the orchestra stalls were dealt with 'in a violent, brutal and sexual manner' when they made their presence felt.

Redmond continued to speak: 'Sir Albert Spicer has all his life been a devoted friend of the cause of Irish freedom.' At this point more women, involved in 'fisticuffs' with the stewards, were ejected from the auditorium with one of the women carried out despite her resistance by holding on to one of the theatre curtains, which she succeeded in pulling down. The whole scene became pandemonium and in a leader feature in the *Kingsland and Hackney Gazette* it was described thus: 'A casual visitor to the Dalston Theatre on Saturday afternoon might have been pardoned for thinking that the pantomime season had commenced somewhat before its time.'

Redmond delivered his judgement on the whole proceedings two days later in *The Times*: 'It seems to me rather tragic that a cause which in the minds and hearts of a great many people is a great cause should be turned into a comic interlude of this description.' In 1913 a cartoon from the *Irish Citizen* depicted a triumphant Redmond, standing over the bound and fallen body of a suffragette, holds a scroll with the words: 'HURRO! FOR LIBERTY!!! NO IRISH WOMAN NEED APPLY – NO VOTES FOR WOMEN BY ORDER – THE NEW LIBERATOR'.

* * *

No. 4 Clapton Common, from a postcard *c.* 1910. This substantial house was the Training College for the Salvation Army. (Hackney Archives)

In 1899, when Charles Booth's social researchers visited Hackney, they commented that in Upper Clapton 'there is a marked absence of public houses and poor streets'. On the resulting 'Poverty Maps' that depicted the overall nature of the area, Clapton Common was coloured yellow with a little red, indicating wealthy occupants. This was the best possible social category, confirming the high social status of the common at the end of the 19th century and making it one of the richest areas in Hackney. Unlike other parts of the borough, Upper Clapton and Stamford Hill remained select well into the early 20th century.

Prosperous families had flocked here since the beginning of the 19th century, and particularly in the 1870s and '80s after a number of detached and semi-detached smaller villas were built along the eastern and northern side of the common. In 1880, William Booth, the founder of the Salvation Army, purchased No. 114 Clapton Common for the substantial sum of £1,260. This house was apparently 'longed for' by his wife Catherine and William recorded how 'they look on to the Common, and the tram-cars passing in the distance, the children at play, the cows grazing, dogs swimming about the pond, all together make the outlook quite lively'. In 1912 Elizabeth Fry, the prison reformer, also wanted to buy another house on the common, No. 22, to establish a women's refuge, but according to the local press it was seen as a threat to high-class property values.

The Booths had moved from Whitechapel in 1868 first to South Hackney, and then in 1880 going further northwards to the leafy suburbs of Upper Clapton. This was also the route taken by successful Jewish immigrants. In the early 19th century Nathan Meyer Rothschild, member of the Rothschild banking dynasty, had lived in Stamford Hill for a short while, as had Joseph Montefiore and the Goldsmid family. 'Among the larger houses standing in their own grounds in Stamford Hill … resided years ago, men who may have made themselves famous in the mercantile and financial world … Some of our most opulent Jews, such as Rothschild and Goldsmid and others.'

By the end of the 19th century the Jewish population in Britain had grown significantly as a result of the violence shown towards the Jews in the Ukraine, Poland, Lithuania and Russia. These vicious anti-Jewish riots, known as *pogroms*, escalated to intolerable proportions between 1881 and 1914. Mobs regularly attacked houses, businesses and synagogues leaving tens of thousands dead and millions without homes or livelihoods. More than two million Jews emigrated during this period, heading mainly for America, with some coming to England.

By 1901 approximately 150,000 Jews were living in England with an estimated 120,000 in London and 100,000 settled in Spitalfields and neighbouring Whitechapel. Attracted by cheap housing and existing synagogues, built in the early 19th century by anglicised Jews, these immigrants found work in the rag and furniture trades and in local markets. At the turn of the 20th century it is estimated that in the Wentworth Street district of Spitalfields the population was 95% Jewish.

As early as 1872 the Jewish community had identified that: 'In the interests of Anglo-Jewry as a whole … the decentralisation of East End Jewry is most urgently demanded … . The Jewish problem is the East End problem.' But little happened immediately. Many Jews felt comfortable and at home in Whitechapel with shops, religious facilities and work on their doorstep. By the turn of the 20th century, a Dispersion Committee had been set up, stressing that the only way to accelerate the process of decentralisation of the Jews would be 'by the provision of sufficient religious facilities'.

In the 1880s Jewish traders and artisans who had found financial success and did not want to remain in the 'ghetto' started to move further north to South Hackney, Stamford Hill and Stoke Newington. By this time there were in the region of 5,000 Jews in Hackney and in 1895 the area was described as 'thickly populated by the better class of Jewish working man.' Moving from Whitechapel was also actively encouraged by the Four Per Cent Industrial Dwellings Company Ltd, who built a number of affordable mansion blocks in these areas. Founded by Nathaniel Mayer Rothschild in 1885, this philanthropic organisation raised funds by issuing shares to investors, who were guaranteed a 4% return. Coronation and Imperial Avenues (1903) and Navarino Mansions (1905) were built to provide 'the industrial classes with commodious and healthy dwellings at a minimum rent'. Both these blocks were designed by the venerable Nathan Solomon Joseph. Navarino Mansions, on Dalston Lane, comprises four six-storey blocks orientated north to south to take full advantage of the sun. With attractive landscaped courtyards these red brick blocks, topped by steeply pitched, French hipped slated roofs, were originally designed to house 300 people.

Dalston, Stoke Newington and Stamford Hill's suburban charm 'began to attract a constant drip-drip of Jewish immigrants, which soon grew into a steady stream and ultimately into a copious flood'. In response to this copious flood a number of synagogues began to appear. In 1897, Hackney Synagogue in Brenthouse Road (formerly known as Devonshire Road) was built to the designs of Delissa Joseph, nephew to Nathan. In 1901 it was also decided to build a larger synagogue in Stoke Newington to accommodate the eagerly anticipated residents of Coronation and Imperial Avenues. In the *Jewish Chronicle* it was reported that Jews: 'would now be willing to migrate knowing the existence of such a place of worship where they can send their children to receive a religious education'.

In January 1912 a meeting of the United Synagogue took place where it was controversially decided to relocate the New Synagogue to Stamford Hill. This decision was not popular as 'the largest number of New Synagogue members now resided in the East End'. A power struggle ensued between the wealthier and more prosperous members of the United Synagogue and those from working-class backgrounds. The members in favour of Stamford Hill argued that 'some 600-800 children in the Stamford Hill, Tottenham and Clapton areas were not receiving any Hebrew or Religious education whatsoever'.

The Ark with its ornate canopy in Clapton Federation Synagogue, which was demolished in 2006. (Nigel Corrie/English Heritage)

When a compromise was suggested, in the form of the synagogue located in South Tottenham, near to Clapton and Stamford Hill, where there was a higher need among the working-class Jew, many of the more affluent Jews found this untenable: 'we cannot and will not have the New Synagogue placed in Tottenham'.

In the end, at a cost of more than £20,000, the United Synagogue Council resolved to build the 'new'

New Synagogue in Egerton Road, Stamford Hill – at the heart of the wealthy Ashkenazi community. Designed by Nathan's son, Ernest Martin Joseph, the synagogue and its neighbouring school were built in an Edwardian Baroque style. The interior copied the apse and galleries of the original synagogue in Bishopsgate in the City of London, incorporating some of its original fittings including the mahogany Ark of 1838. In 1915 it was reported that at the opening ceremony the Mayor of Stoke Newington spoke of: 'how glad he was that the Jewish Community had followed the example of the Gentile migration to that area'.

With the influx into Hackney of people from all rural areas of England, together with the Jews it became increasingly necessary to improve health-care provision. Before the Jews arrived, the largest immigrant group was German, arriving mainly after the Hanoverian accession to the British throne in 1714. By the 1880s it was believed that the German population in London was in the region of 40,000 people. In order to avoid burdening the host country and any consequent ill-feeling, it was customary for affluent émigrés, like the Jews and Germans, to provide social and health-care for their community. During the 19th century a number of purpose-built hospitals were constructed, including the German Hospital (1845), Eastern Fever Hospital (1870) and Metropolitan Hospital (from 1888 on Kingsland Road). There was also an expansion and improvement of former workhouse infirmaries, such as Hackney Hospital (1750) and St Leonard's Hospital (1774). In the 1880s approximately 10% of the patients at the German Hospital were Jewish. According to Michael Bernstein, author of *Stamford Hill and the Jews*, the Jewish community preferred the German to the London Hospital, as it was easier for patients to converse with the German staff. Despite this, it was discovered that the Conversionist Society had been attempting 'to entrap the Jewish sick' through evangelist proselytising. In 1894 a case was reported involving a 'pious old Jew' whose prayer book had been substituted by a Protestant Bible. At a public meeting it was decided that Jewish support should be transferred to the Metropolitan Hospital, which by 1896 had allocated 12 of its 60 beds to Jewish patients with access to a Jewish physician and a cook who prepared kosher food. On 18 April 1912 *The Times* reported that Arthur Sassoon, a Jewish merchant banker, had left it £2,000, such was the dedication of the Jewish community to the hospital.

On the other side of borough the Salvation Army was practising another kind of religious dedication, but this time directed towards unmarried mothers. The Salvation Army fervently believed that these women needed special spiritual and social support if they were to avoid being drawn into prostitution.

On 4 July 1912 Princess Louise, daughter of Queen Victoria, laid the foundation stone for a new building for the Salvation Army's Mothers' Hospital. From 1890 the Salvation Army had been providing maternity services to unmarried women in Ivy

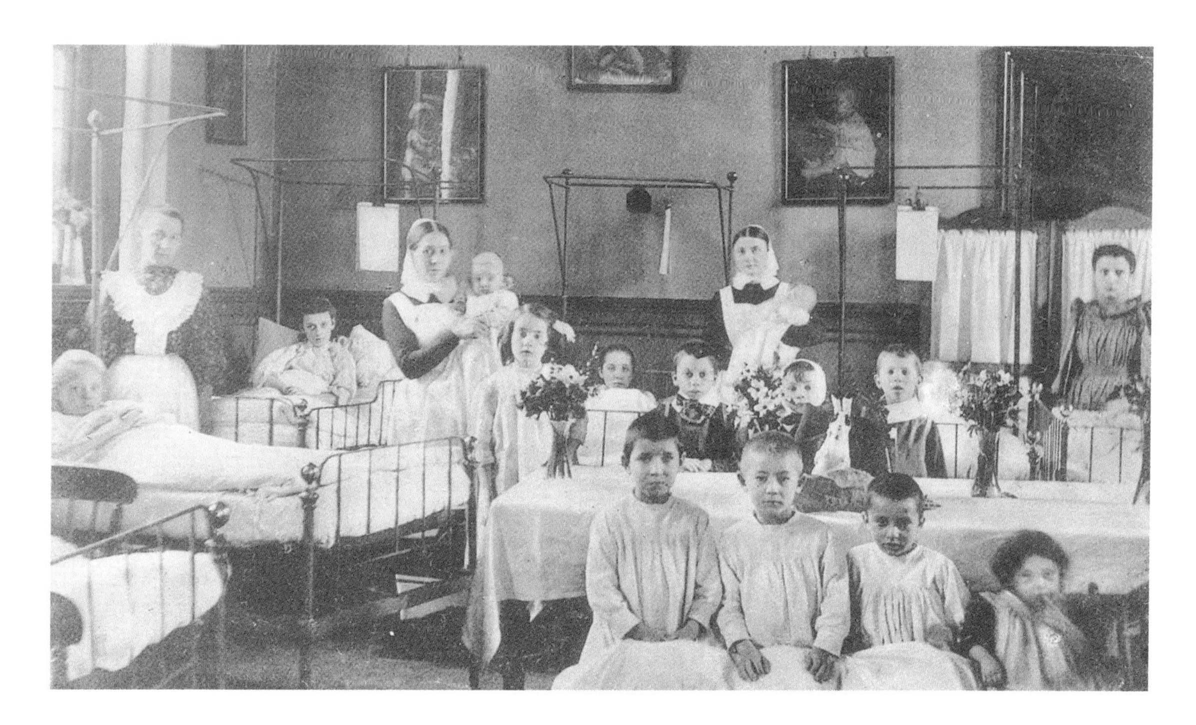

House, a large, Georgian terraced house located on the north corner of Richmond Road at 271 Mare Street. Initially, it was a joint rescue home and hospital for unmarried mothers, but by 1895 it had became a maternity hospital.

The head of the Salvation Army Women's social services, Mrs Florence Bramwell Booth, daughter-in-law of William and Catherine, asked Captain Frost, a midwife from Guernsey, to manage the organisation's rescue homes for unmarried mothers. Demand for their services had grown rapidly and it soon became apparent that a new facility was needed. In 1906 a detailed report by the London County Council described Ivy House as consisting of a basement, ground floor and two floors above. The basement housed a kitchen, kitchen offices, dining room and bathroom for domestic staff. The ground floor held the dining room for midwife pupils and for nursing staff, which doubled up as a lecture theatre, two administration offices, a room used in connection with district work, and a convalescent ward. There was a day nursery, lying-in wards, a labour room, night nursery and an ante-natal room, which acted as a receiving room. Altogether there were six wards with 12 cots and 22 beds. There was no bathroom for the patients – instead movable baths were used.

The children's ward in the German Hospital, *c.*1910. (Hackney Archives)

Florence Booth and her assistant, Commissioner Adelaide Cox began to see the need to separate unmarried mothers from the ordinary rescue cases because of their special circumstances. Ivy House was intended for 'girls who previous to their fall, have led respectable lives, and who have been betrayed by the so-called men to whom they have been engaged and whom they loved not wisely, but too well'. But as with all their 'rescue work' nurses combined delivering babies with evangelising the mothers. The nurses did not leave the patients without a prayer and 'some straight dealing with them about their souls'. The new hospital on Lower Clapton Road was to cater for all kinds of mothers with wards for married, unmarried, Jewish and special cases. In *The Times* it was reported that additional money needed to be raised towards the costs, but that: 'Substantial help was afforded by a legacy left by a Mrs Lewis Hill, a Jewish lady.'

General William Booth and his wife, Catherine Booth, had had a long association with Hackney, as noted above, making it their home from 1868 as well as basing here the headquarters of their very successful brand of Protestant Christianity. After its missionary beginnings in Whitechapel in 1878, the Army's focus soon moved towards Hackney and Clapton where many inhabitants were in need of both spiritual guidance and poor relief. By the early 1880s the Salvation Army had outgrown its premises in Whitechapel and required a larger place for worship and training in Clapton. In *c.*1882 the Booths converted the former London Orphan Asylum in Linscott Road into a hall that could seat 4,700 people. The wings of the building became a training barracks – including classrooms, workrooms and bedrooms – that could accommodate 150 male and 150 female cadets at a time, all of whom were committed to furthering the Salvation Army's mission.

Such was the Salvation Army's success that by 1903 it was attracting 1,635 worshippers to evening Sunday service, far outstripping other places of worship in the area. But it would be a mistake to think they were popular with everyone. A local policeman in the 1890s remarked: 'the district is the stronghold of the Army. The Salvationists have drummed all the best people away.' In 1910 the Mayor of Hackney, T.E. Young, Mrs Bramwell Booth and Adelaide Cox laid three foundation stones for the Women's Social Work Headquarters of the Salvation Army at 280 Mare Street, which opened in 1913, along with the Mothers' Hospital.

Sadly William Booth did not witness these two important events as he died on 20 August 1912. Two days later a procession carried his body from his home in Hadley Wood in Enfield to the Congress Hall in Clapton. Arriving shortly before midnight, the car took the coffin to the rear of the hall to avoid the hundreds of people who had waited for hours at the main entrance. The body lay in state for four days with a glass panel placed over the head of the coffin so that the many mourners could take a last look at this remarkable man. On Saturday, 24 August 1912 it was estimated that 50,000 mourners passed through the Congress Hall.

Originally the public was to be admitted from 10am to 10pm, but it was reported in *The Times* that the hall had been opened at 5.30am to cope with the numbers who wanted to pay their respects. 'The long procession scarcely paused throughout the day and never really stopped … . It was a cosmopolitan crowd; there were to be seen Bengali women and Chinese women in native costume, a coloured minister from the United States, old Salvationists from distant parts of the country, labouring men and clerks, seamstresses, Boy Scouts, policemen and ministers of every denomination.'

The funeral service was held on 28 August 1912 at Olympia with the burial taking place the following day. The route of the procession travelled along Victoria Embankment to the City and up to Kingsland Road to Stoke Newington and the Abney Park Cemetery, reaching its gates at about 3pm. A banner spread across Stoke Newington High Street bore the words: 'The Metropolitan Boroughs of Hackney and Stoke Newington mourn the loss of a noble life.' On the coffin were the 'General's cap, his Bible, Song-book, and Soldier's Guide, a volume containing a portion of scripture for each day of the year'.

* * *

Life in Hackney was not all hardship. Even working-class families could now gain an education and have time to read books and journals. After the Public Libraries Acts in 1903, Hackney Council bought land in Mare Street for a central library. Designed by Henry Crouch, it was built with funds from Andrew Carnegie, and opened in 1908.

The Dalston Branch Library, also a gift from Andrew Carnegie, was opened on 26 October 1912. Located on the corner of Forest Road and Woodland Road, it was designed by Edwin Cooper, who two years previously had set up his own architectural practice.

The Council had also commissioned Cooper to design Clapton Branch library in Northwold Road (extant), and Homerton Branch library (extant as Chats Palace). Cooper, a follower of the fashionable Beaux-Arts Movement, had consolidated his technique for competition designs for large buildings with the use of signature detailing in the form of colonnades and rich ornamental detailing. Built on land given by the Rhodes family, who also funded an athletics club next door, Dalston library was built by Messrs J.E.Whiter & Co who were congratulated on 'having produced a building which is a distinct ornament to the neighbourhood'.

It cost an estimated £5,280 and included a simple Doric colonnade that ran around the perimeter and a Greek-style portico and loggia forming the focal point and entrance to the library. Above the portico was a louvred cupola with a flèche. Inside, the library could accommodate 64 in the reading- and magazine-room and contained enough storage for

The Prince and Princess of Wales, later George V and Queen Mary, accompanied by the cavalry, en route to open the Central Library in 1908. On the left is the old Town Hall, on the right, the Hackney Empire. (Hackney Archives)

21,000 volumes. It also had 'ample accommodation' for newspaper readers and a room dedicated to 'juvenile' readers.

The *Hackney and Kingsland Gazette* reported that libraries were to: 'encourage people who did not read, to read, and to encourage those who did read to extend the scope of their reading and quality of the books which they studied'. Mr A.J.Shepheard, of the London County Council, hoped that the Library Committee 'would not be discouraged if the books taken out were of the lightest description. It was very difficult to get a certain class of person to read at all, but if they once started to read books of fiction they would later on ascend to something better'.

The North-East London Institute, at Nos. 236-238 Dalston Lane, occupied enlarged premises on the site of the former Dalston School of Industry, which had opened in 1790. In 1904 plans by the architect Arthur W. Cooksey were drawn up for two new blocks to accommodate mechanical and electrical engineering workshops, metalworking workshops and science laboratories for inorganic chemistry, physics, physical chemistry, optics and biological sciences. In 1909 this institute was transferred to the London County Council along with the South Hackney Technical Institute on Cassland Road, which later became known as the Sir John Cass's Hackney Institute. There was also an Art School at 81 Clapton Common. Training for art teachers was provided along with day and evening classes for pupils. The school closed in 1916 after the LCC withdrew its support.

When not bettering themselves through education, the people of Hackney, Shoreditch and Stoke Newington spent their leisure time watching

Dalston Branch Library on the corner of Forest and Woodland Roads, *c.*1912. The building was destroyed by a V2 Bomb in January 1945. (Hackney Archives)

Postcard showing the bandstand in Clissold Park, *c.*1910, with the new church of St Mary's, Stoke Newington, in the background. (Hackney Archives)

variety shows at the large number of theatres and music halls that had sprung up in the 19th and early 20th centuries. Many of the music halls were literally rooms in local pubs, others were grander establishments like the Shoreditch Empire (1856), the Britannia Theatre (1858), Hoxton Hall (1863), the Alexandra Theatre (1897), the Dalston Theatre (1898) and Hackney Empire (1901). The Hackney Empire, designed by Frank Matcham, has recently been restored to its former flamboyant glory. It was commissioned by the theatre entrepreneur Oswald Stoll, who not only strove to provide entertainment in establishments built to the highest architectural standards, but also to attract a more 'respectable' audience to music hall.

One music-hall performer who drew a fine line between respectability and vulgarity was the famous Marie Lloyd, whose real name was Matilda Wood. Born in Hoxton in 1870 she started singing, aged 14, at the Grecian Music Hall which was attached to the Eagle Tavern on City Road. Her father, John Wood, was a part-time waiter there and it was he who encouraged her to study the singers and artistes of the time. Initially appearing as Bella Delmere, she soon adopted the stage name Marie Lloyd, first appearing under this name in June 1884 at the Falstaff Music Hall in Deptford. That night launched her career. As well as her bawdy numbers, she sang of the hardships endured by those who, like her, had lived in the slums of Hoxton. Songs like 'My Old Man Said Follow the Van' resonated with her working-class audience.

Her meteoric rise was not without controversy. In 1896, aged 26, she met the singer Alec Hurley but was not able to marry him until his divorce came through in 1906. Four years later she left Hurley to live with a well-known jockey, Bernard Dillon.

Their life together was fraught with difficulties. Dillon became an alcoholic after losing his jockey's licence, and Lloyd, with her scandalous lifestyle and risqué songs, was not invited to take part in the inaugural Royal Command Performance in July 1912. This snub drove her to organise a rival performance in a nearby theatre, which she advertised was 'by command of the British public'.

In October 1913 she and Dillon left for America, describing themselves as man and wife, but on disembarking they were threatened with deportation and sent back to Ellis Island. On 3 October 1913 *The Times* reported that 'Mr Dillon is charged with having brought an alien into the country to whom he is not married.' Eventually they were allowed to stay as long as they lived apart. This difficult arrangement lasted until February 1914 when they married after the death of Lloyd's husband Alec Hurley. Eight years later Marie Lloyd also died of heart and kidney failure, at the age of 52.

* * *

Just as the world's impoverished people came to Hackney, Hackney's poor also began to be able to view the world through the public projection of celluloid. The Cinematograph Act of 1909 was introduced to regulate the film industry, followed by the establishment of the British Board of Film Censors. The moving image was fast becoming the most popular form of entertainment. By 1912 there were dozens of 'cinematographs' or cinemas in the borough. Early examples included Henry Mason's cinematograph at No. 329 Mare Street and the Premier Rink in Clapton. By 1910 the Hackney Empire had started to show films and the Clapton Cinematograph was opened on Lower Clapton Road. Other cinemas included Moss Empire's Stoke Newington Palace, the Hackney Picture Palace at No. 331 Mare Street and the Dalston Picture Theatre at Nos. 17-19 Dalston Lane. Among London's grandest was the Hackney Pavilion at No. 290 Mare Street. Designed by George Billings and opened in 1914, it could seat 1,162 in an ornate auditorium 'the equal of any Edwardian theatre'.

From 1910, Pathé News was producing cinema newsreels to be shown prior to feature films. In 1912 the people of Hackney would have witnessed in uncanny silence the return of Captain Scott's ship the *Terra Nova*; the bravado of the Wright Brothers giving Theodore Roosevelt a ride in their plane at an air show in St Louis, Missouri; the shocking conditions endured by civilian refugees in the war-torn Balkans; and the rescue of 327 survivors from the icy wastes of the Atlantic Ocean after the passenger liner, *RMS Titanic*, hit an iceberg and sank off the coast of Newfoundland on 15 April 1912.

One thousand, five hundred and twenty-three people on the *Titanic* perished that day, amongst them a 40-year-old second-class saloon steward, James Thomas Wood from Narford Road, Upper

E-ARE-ACKNOWLEDGED
AS
THE
MOST
UP TO DATE
ANIMATED PICTURE
PRODUCERS
IN
THE WORLD
ELECTRIC PICTURE PALACE
INTERESTING AMUSING & INSTRUCTIVE
BILL STICKERS WILL BE PROSECUTED
CHERI-BIBI
Miss HENNY PORTEN
CHÉRI-BIBI
HACKNEY PICTURE PALACE
LATEST WAR NEWS
WAR NEWS
HENNY PORTEN
HACKNEY FURNIS
COMPY LIM
BRANCH SHOW R
HACKNE
FOR THE KING

Clapton. He had only intended to help on board before the *Titanic* set sail, but by some cruel twist of fate he was persuaded to sign on as second-class steward for the ship's maiden voyage. Among the third-class passengers, many of whom were leaving the squalor of London to start new lives in America was 44-year-old John George Sage, his wife Annie and their nine children. John and his wife were born in Hackney in the 1860s and around the turn of the century moved with their children to the East of England. John then travelled to North America, discovering Florida and resolving to move his family there. Putting a deposit on a farm, he returned home in late 1911 to prepare his family for the move. According to Julia Lafferty, who has researched local peoples' link to the *Titanic*, his wife was reluctant to leave England, but had been persuaded by John's enthusiasm for 'a lovely plot of land' that he had found in Jacksonville. Lafferty says: '[Annie] had a fear of water following an incident during which her daughter Dorothy had fallen into a well in the backyard of the family home and almost drowned'. On the 10 April 1912 the family boarded the *Titanic* at Southampton, having sent their furniture and the family piano on ahead.

Despite the opening up of the world, it took almost a year for the news of Captain Scott's death and that of his companions to reach England from the frozen wilderness of Antarctica. They had perished in the spring of 1912, but news of the tragedy only reached London in February 1913.

The year before, the news of Amundsen's triumph in reaching the South Pole became known to the world. When the victorious Norwegian, by now crowned the greatest Polar explorer of his age, stopped off in London on his way home in November 1912, the 'reception he received was far from warm'.

Pastimes in 1912 included pigeon shooting and there were a number of rifle clubs. At the 1912 Summer Olympics in Stockholm, William Percy Grosvenor, who was born in Dalston in 1869, won a silver medal as part of the British clay pigeon team. Other popular sports included gymnastics with the Orion Hall in East Bank and the Boys' Institute in Woodland Road founded by the Rhodes family, which included a gymnasium and rifle range.

Henry Allingham, who became for one month the oldest living man in the world in 2009, was born on 6 June 1896 at Hackney Wick, near the site of the London 2012 Summer Olympics. The year of his birth coincided with the first modern Olympic Games in Athens. Allingham's sport was rowing, to which he was introduced by his mother's youngest brother. At the Eton Mission Rowing Club at the end of Wallis Road, he became a regular on the water from 1909 until he left for the First World War. Having survived the Battle of Jutland, the Somme and Ypres, he returned to row in 1919. He once said: 'I thought I couldn't row properly and I learned to row here and got better and better. I got all the books out of the libraries. I got a lot of pleasure out of rowing and just watching people rowing'. In 2008, at the age of 112,

The Hackney Picture Palace in 1914, with the railway bridge over Mare Street to the right and Graham Road to the left. (Hackney Archives)

Henry Allingham was the guest of honour at the Eton Mission Rowing Club.

The Eton Mission and its breakaway rival, the Eton Manor Boys' Club, were philanthropic organisations that defined the spirit of the age. The intention of the Eton Mission was never ambiguous. It was to 'help the people of Hackney Wick to Heaven; and if they are not interested in Heaven, to help them to make the best of this life, anyway'. Described as 'a queer mixture of religion, sport and social service', the Eton Manor was responsible for much of Hackney's sporting heritage. In 1889, Reverend E.K.Douglas, from the Eton Mission, appealed to the Metropolitan Public Gardens Association to use its influence to get permission for the boys to play football on the Marshes. During the second half of the 19th century 'association' football had become a popular sport among all social classes. Originally the Eton Mission Boys' Club played football in Victoria Park, but the numbers of 'boys' who wanted to play the game far outstripped the number of pitches available, so they played on the marshes. This resulted in cattle and sheep drovers confiscating

Joseph Wilberforce and Gertrude Richardson on a tandem, 1919. Mr Wilberforce and Mrs Richardson were organisers of the Orchard Mission in Well Street. (Hackney Archives)

the goal posts in an attempt to drive them off the common land. The Board of Agriculture responded to Douglas' appeal by agreeing to place the marshes under the control of the London County Council. The LCC, the Hackney District Board and other individuals purchased the land for £75,000 from the Lord of the Manor and its other owners, and in 1894, Hackney Marshes was dedicated as a public open space. The Marshes proved so popular that Eton Mission had to instigate the marking and booking of pitches, which created the 'largest area of marked-out football pitches in the world'.

* * *

The year 1912 has been described as 'the defiant swansong' before Britain moved inexorably towards the Great War. That horrific event would change the social landscape of the whole nation, and of Hackney, forever. The years just prior to 1912 established the concepts of state-funded welfare and social justice, and many of the ideas from this period are still relevant today.

The Eton Manor Otters swimming team posed in front of their club house in Hackney Wick, *c.*1918. (Hackney Archives)

Hackney: 2012

Julliet Gardiner and David Garrard

In the long, far from hot summer of 2011, Hackney briefly exploded. Riots, disturbances and looting erupted over two nights in a narrow sector in the heart of the borough. Shop windows were smashed, goods plundered, cars set alight. Hackney inevitably took its place in the news agenda as 'one of the poorest boroughs in Britain', the home of the deprived, the dispossessed and the alienated. Yet by morning there was a different story, of community action with residents and officials coming together to clean up the detritus, repair damage, support and reimburse those whose livelihood had been wrenched away. Brooms, mops and 'I Love Hackney' tee shirts replaced iron bars, hooded tops and masked faces. Once again Hackney proved a near textbook example of inner-city living.

For more than a century, decay, dereliction and delinquency have co-existed with local pride, optimism and progress. The borough is a double Janus: looking west towards Islington, east towards Essex, down the hill towards the City and north towards London's outer suburbs. Its pockets of extreme deprivation have been offset by remarkable buildings, generous open spaces, settled residential communities and radical hopes. The London Borough of Hackney, created in its present form in 1965 by linking the former Metropolitan Boroughs of Shoreditch, Hackney and Stoke Newington, remains firmly embedded in the inner city: cosmopolitan, vibrant, sometimes troubled, ever changing, with affinities with the East End, yet separate from the mass of Stepney, Whitechapel, Plaistow, Canning Town, West Ham … .

In recent years Hackney has had its own high-profile residents turned biographers, its Boswell, its metropolitan Cobbett, its Jack London, restlessly roaming the threatened heartlands, the fraying edgelands. Patrick Wright and Iain Sinclair have put Hackney in the centre of the map of urban degeneration and regeneration, of imperilled communities, of lost authenticities and eroded localisms. Yet to a large extent Hackney's high streets remain resolutely uncloned, its open spaces are mostly unencroached upon and its architectural heritage robustly defended: the borough's housing disasters show signs of redemption and its educational needs seem to have been gradually grasped, even as its social mix has remained shifting

Street party in Daubeney Road, Clapton, to celebrate the Armistice, November 1918. (Hackney Archives)

and fluid. And, a rarity among local authorities, it has a directly elected mayor.

How to arrive at this point? How to recount the story of Hackney's last century in a few thousand words? How to find a thread running true from the First World War to the London Olympics of 2012 through one of the capital's poorest, troubled, most diverse, most innovative boroughs? The best we can do, perhaps, is to trace a few essential themes – housing, employment, culture, the changes wrought by war and immigration – that figure most prominently in the district's recent history, observing as we go how these intersect both with the lives of individual residents and communities, and also with broader contemporary currents in the history of the metropolis, and of the nation as a whole.

* * *

In May 1915 the German Kaiser, Wilhelm II, who had expressly forbidden air attacks on London at the start of the Great War, relaxed his strictures and permitted bombing east of the Tower of London. On 31 May the first bombs to fall on London – simple metal canisters wrapped in tar-impregnated rope and containing a mixture of thermite, tar and benzol activated by a fuse – dropped on 16 Alkham Road, Stoke Newington. The eerie, cigar-shaped zeppelins then flew south, dropping 21 incendiaries on the Shoreditch Empire Music Hall. In total there were 20 air raids on Britain in 1915, killing 181 people and injuring 455. Anti-aircraft guns were stationed in Victoria Park and gradually grew more effective, if not in hitting enemy aircraft, then at least in compelling them to fly higher.

Ida Rex was a teacher at Shap Street elementary school in Haggerston in 1915. A year later Miss Rex was transferred to Laburnum Road Boys' School near the canal bridge in Haggerston because most of the male teachers 'had gone to the front'. She taught 'geography combined with science', and every time the air raid sounded, had to get all the boys down from the top of the school to the cellar 'with the guns going. I was very scared … we sang going down to drown the sound of the guns. One morning we arrived to find the windows broken. A bomb had been dropped in a brickyard by the canal and part had gone into our school and damaged all one corner. So the school was shut down and we told the children they could go off for the day … the raids were very bad then.' There was no government-sponsored evacuation in the First World War, so working-class pupils were obliged to sit out the air attacks. Over 8,000 civilians in Britain were killed in air raids during the war.

Miss Rex was living with two friends in a Salvation Army Boarding House in Clapton Square:

We three were very scared. We had one room between us at the top of the house … soldiers were billeted there as well and so we always used to put the table and chairs in front of the door as well as trying to lock it. Then we had to move everything when the sirens went and rush downstairs in our dressing gowns, there was never time for anything else . . . . Once when we were coming downstairs we heard cheers and cheers because a Zeppelin was coming down at Cuffley . . . it was just like a big cigar in the sky. You could see it going across from our house and all the people were cheering and singing 'Tipperary' . . . .

The war formally ended on the eleventh hour of the eleventh day of the eleventh month in 1918. 'Peace Parties' were held in local streets for the children with cakes and lemonade, flags and bunting, and memorials were erected in memory of the dead in almost every town and village in Britain. Field Marshal Sir William Robertson, Commander in Chief of General Staff from 1916 (and the first man ever to rise to the British Army's highest rank from that of private soldier), was one of the guests present when the plaque on a specially-built hall alongside Stoke Newington Library was dedicated as a war memorial in June 1923. Despite the odd omission and misspelling, the plaque constitutes the most comprehensive record of the war dead of the borough.

Almost exactly ten years after the end of the war, Sir Hubert Llewellyn Smith directed a team of researchers at the London School of Economics to revisit Charles Booth's famous survey conducted at the end of the 19th century. *The New Survey of London Life and Labour* was published in nine volumes between 1930 and 1935. Like Booth, Llewellyn and his team were particularly interested in the extent and causes of poverty. In the words of a contemporary review, 'The New Survey is the Intelligent Man's guide to the mean streets and withered lives of London . . . there is hardly a phase in the life of the five and a half million people of the metropolis which has escaped the zeal of the investigators. In the panorama that spreads before us we may distinguish three prominent landmarks – the standard of living, the manifold ways in which people earn their livelihood and the various pursuits of their leisure hours.' The landmarks that served Llewellyn Smith and his team work well as categories to map the history of the original borough of Hackney in the 20th century and into the 21st.

By 1911, 222,533 people lived in what had recently become the Metropolitan Borough. But this was the population highpoint: by 1921 the number had fallen to 222,142, then to 215,333 ten years later. By 1951 the population was 164,766, and when the three former boroughs joined together in 1965 the trend continued: a combined population of 220,279 in 1971 had fallen to 180,434 ten years later. Today the population of Hackney is on the increase again: the 2001 census put the population at 202,824 while in 2010 estimates vary between 219,000 and 237,646.

Until the First World War at least 80% of Britain's population lived in accommodation provided by private landlords. Sometimes this would be rooms in their landlord's house; some landlords might own a handful of dwellings that they rented out, while others were effectively housing corporations owning large amounts of property. The number of owner-occupiers nationwide in the early 1920s was roughly 1.75%, while local authorities housed around 1% of the population. The remaining housing was provided by employers or by quasi-philanthropic organisations such as the Peabody Trust or Sydney Waterlow's Improved Industrial Dwellings Corporation (IIDC). These had been responsible for the earliest slum clearance programmes in the 1860s and '70s, replacing squalid courts and alleys with tall, Spartan blocks of flats intended to provide working-class families with a minimum standard of accommodation at an affordable rent. Philanthropic housing declined between the wars as its role was gradually taken over by state agencies, although the Four Per Cent Industrial Dwellings Company built at least one remarkable estate during this period: this was Evelyn Court on Amhurst Road, designed by the great inter-war Modernists Burnet, Tait & Lorne, its rows of flat-roofed, white-rendered blocks recalling Berlin or Vienna rather than Hackney Downs.

Local authority provision – 'council housing' – arrived somewhat later on the scene. The 1875 Artisans' and Labourers' Dwellings Act enabled councils to redevelop slum property, but it was not until the formation of the London County Council (LCC) in 1889 that these powers began to be used. Council building increased dramatically in the inter-war years, assisted by legislation such as Arthur Greenwood's 1930 Housing Act, which allocated central government grants for slum clearance. Over 30% of new housing built during these decades was provided by local authorities; this, and a corresponding increase in owner-occupation among the middle classes, meant that the proportion built for rent by private landlords declined to just 20%.

The LCC was still the prime mover, its estates becoming ever larger and more expansively laid out. The style was usually a nostalgic neo-Georgian, but the scale and planning belonged to the modern age. The vast Kingsmead Estate, built on part of Hackney Marshes in 1937, brought the European *zeilenbau* (linear blocks) to the Lea Valley: the 17 five-storey blocks were arranged in long serried rows 'to ensure the maximum of sunlight flooding every room', with a school on site and a park running down the centre. A similarly expansive scheme was the Whitmore Estate around Philipp Street in Haggerston, its 16 blocks given names – Bowyer House, Archer House, Arrow House – 'connected with the ancient sport of archery, which was practised in the neighbourhood in olden times'.

The borough councils, meanwhile, also began to move into housing provision. The first 'borough' housing in London had been built at Moira Place, Shoreditch in 1899: 106 tenements with electric lighting powered by the newly-inaugurated Coronet Street waste incinerator. Hackney followed suit in the 1920s, at first with maisonettes like the 48 built in Fletching Road, and later with LCC-style blocks designed by the housing specialists Messrs Joseph

Dire housing: Clarence Cottages behind Clapton Square, in the 1930s. (Hackney Archives)

(the firm established by Nathan Joseph, architect of Navarino Mansions). By 1939 Hackney had completed 13 estates and provided 2,780 housing units. Suburban Stoke Newington, by contrast, had built a mere 304 dwellings, most of them on the big Lordship Road Estate, completed in 1934.

Hackney was badly bombed during the Second World War and large swathes of the borough were destroyed or damaged beyond repair. The worst attack took place on the night of 13/14 October 1940 when a bomb fell through all five floors of Coronation Avenue, a tenement block at 157-161 Stoke Newington Road. The basement of the building had been designated as a public shelter and people were trapped when fallen debris blocked the exits, a water main burst flooded the basement and fire broke out. One hundred and twenty-three people lost their lives that night and a memorial in Abney Park Cemetery lists their names. Hackney's relative proximity to the London docks, a priority target for the Luftwaffe, meant that the borough suffered considerable aerial attrition throughout the Blitz. By May 1941, 2,490 homes in the borough of Hackney had been destroyed or demolished, as had 2,955 in Shoreditch and 246 in Stoke Newington; 650 Hackney, 1,136 Shoreditch and 322 Stoke Newington residents had been killed or seriously wounded. The respite from the Blitz was short lived. Though most of Hitler's secret weapons – the pilotless 'doodlebug' V1, launched shortly after D-Day in June 1944, and later the V2 rocket – fell south of the Thames, some landed on parts of Hackney. Mrs Barrett, who lived at Sutton Dwellings, Shoreditch, recalled that when her family emerged from their shelter after a 'buzz bomb' fell nearby, it was into:

A pall, a solid pall [of dust] like the thickest pea-souper [fog] that you've ever seen ... there was all this screaming ... when we eventually got up to our flat, all the walls were down and falling across the passage and all the windows were out ... glass was all over the place, and the doors were blown off their hinges and my mother had got some geraniums out on the balcony and bits of these was all embedded in the paintwork on the balconies and all that was left of the curtains was a fringe 'cause they were all lace curtains then, they'd been sucked out into the ruins.

Fortunately the main impact of the bomb was on a row of unoccupied slum flats awaiting demolition, and though there were injuries from falling masonry and flying glass, no one was killed.

The post-war reconstruction of London was governed by the LCC's County of London Plan of 1943, often referred to as the Abercrombie Plan after its co-author, the town planner Patrick Abercrombie. The brief was to address the problems of traffic congestion, inadequate open spaces, the jumble of housing and industry and the persistence of overcrowded and dilapidated slum dwellings. Its recommendations included building new towns to 'decant', in the words of the report, the surplus population of the overcrowded areas, throwing a green belt around London to arrest urban sprawl, and introducing a zoning policy to separate residential and industrial areas. The aim was to reduce the population of the inner London boroughs, but for the remaining residents the problem of inadequate and outdated housing had still to be addressed; this entailed an enormous house-building programme, to be implemented by the LCC in conjunction with the metropolitan boroughs. In Hackney, the division of responsibility was marked by the North London Line, with the LCC building its estates to the south and the borough council working in the area to the north.

Housing was the political priority in the immediate post-war years. According to Henry Goodrich, the leader of Hackney Council in 1945: 'the people of this country were looking more anxiously at the housing question than anything else'. They were still anxious four years later when, in the run-up to the 1949 borough elections, there were noisy protests in the council chamber at the slow rate of housing provision. However, by 1951 the programme had accelerated, and Hackney was to become the second most active borough in London in terms of housing provision, building 5,864 permanent dwellings in the period to 1961. In addition, there were almost 5,000 temporary 'prefab' homes on rubble-cleared bomb sites such as Trowbridge Road, Prince Edward Road, Chalgrove Road and on the site of what is now a Tesco supermarket in Morning Lane.

In Shoreditch there were fewer but larger new developments since there were more derelict bomb sites to build on. The Colville, Kingsland, St Mary's, Pitfield and Wenlock Barn estates were all built at this time. Wenlock Barn covered 32 acres and contained 944 dwellings, although this fell far short of the near-total reconstruction of the entire borough envisaged under the Abercrombie Plan. Meanwhile, even in Stoke Newington the council started to build in greater quantities, bringing the total number of borough dwellings to 1,973 by 1961.

Much thought went into planning these new estates. Developments often included community halls and tenants' meeting rooms, with communal workshops and recreation spaces on the larger estates and storage space allocated for prams and bicycles. Hackney Council was particularly forward-looking, and in the years immediately after the war, appointed a number of young architects – including Frederick Gibberd, chief architect of Harlow New Town, and later of Liverpool's Roman Catholic Cathedral – to build small, village-like estates that would embody the variety and sense of humanity visibly absent from the monolithic tenement blocks of the inter-war years.

The most celebrated of these pilot developments was the Somerford estate on Shacklewell Lane (1945-7), designed by Gibberd in the cheerful, homely, slightly quaint idiom that was the approved housing vernacular of the Festival of Britain. With its variety of housing types – almshouse-like single-storey cottages for pensioners, two-storey terraces containing both houses and maisonettes, and three-storey blocks, as well as a library and community centre – Somerford epitomised the then-novel principle of 'mixed development', intended both to satisfy a range of housing needs and ensure a lively, informal townscape. The buildings are picturesquely arranged in interlocking squares and courts, and the carefully contrived cross-vistas and juxtapositions of scale have a charm that present-day neglect cannot obliterate.

At the opposite extreme was the LCC's giant Woodberry Down estate in Stoke Newington (1946-52), which housed 6,350 people in 1,765 dwellings and included a community centre, a health centre, primary and secondary schools and a shopping parade. This too was an example of 'mixed' development, with five different housing types spread across its 45 acres, but here the tallest blocks – built of mass concrete due to post-war steel shortages – rose to an unprecedented eight storeys. Despite its amenities, from the parkland setting on the banks of the Stoke Newington Reservoirs to the electric lifts, central heating and cooking facilities in the blocks themselves, Woodberry Down found

few admirers. Architects decried its 'unimaginative' layout and 'coarse' detailing, while local residents were suspicious about the mass importation of slum dwellers, and the right-wing press muttered darkly about political gerrymandering on the part of the Labour-controlled LCC.

High-rise blocks like those at Woodberry Down were a source of contention throughout the second half of the century. Hackney council had announced in 1948 that it would not build above three storeys again – a policy it broadly stuck to until the mid-1950s. However, material circumstances conspired against this resolve. Zoning had restricted the amount of space available for house-building, so that land was scarce and expensive; low-rise developments were considered to take up too much room, leaving insufficient green spaces for the residents. Demographic changes – smaller families, more divorced couples – meant that extra households were created.

Housing on the Somerford Grove Estate, *c.*1948.

At the same time, London was an employment magnet, particularly in the white-collar sector, resulting in an influx of mainly young, single people requiring housing. Industrial or 'system' construction using prefabricated concrete panels allowed what the *Evening News* exaggeratedly described in November 1962 as 'rapid housing – homes put up in less time than it takes to eat lunch'. In 1955 the Conservative Minister for Housing, Duncan Sandys, proposed a subsidy to councils rising for each floor above six storeys; the higher the block, the greater the subsidy, to reflect greater construction costs. The architects themselves contributed to the pressure, inspired by the soaring visions of their Continental and US gurus to design ever taller blocks: Gibberd's Beckers estate on Rectory Road (1955-8) includes two 11-storey point blocks with dramatic barrel-vaulted rooflines, while the three towers proposed

Nicholl House,
Woodberry Down Estate.
(Inge Clemente)

for the contemporary Trelawney estate, a late scheme by Messrs Joseph, rose gradually from 11 to 15 storeys as the council's enthusiasm gathered pace.

By the beginning of the 1970s, however, thinking about urban housing was beginning to change. The collapse of the 22-storey Ronan Point Tower in the adjoining borough of Newham in 1968 had raised fundamental questions about the safety of prefabricated construction, and there was also the gradual realisation that building high did not necessarily save much space, given the amount of open land required to allow enough light into the flats. Meanwhile, social as well as technical problems were becoming apparent. There were concerns about isolation, crime, maintenance, and the unsuitability of tower blocks for the elderly and those with young children, who could be virtually stranded if lifts broke down or were vandalised – as they frequently were. The Holly Street Estate off Richmond Road, a mixture of high-rise and 'snake' blocks connecting the towers, was particularly notorious. Roofs leaked, walls ran with condensation, there were insect and vermin infestations, and the serpentine corridors encouraged muggings, burglary and vandalism. The future Labour Prime Minister Tony Blair, who was living nearby in Mapledene Road, went canvassing there in the 1980s and later claimed that Holly Street had introduced him to the 'society of fear' where people were too scared to open their doors.

By 2002, 23 tower blocks (defined as residential buildings with more than nine storeys) were demolished across the borough. The first to go in 1988 was the 21-storey Northaird Point on the Trowbridge Estate, Hackney Wick, which had been left as the 'leaning tower of 'Ackney' when the first 'blowdown' failed to complete the job. The estate had suffered long-standing structural and social problems, and Brian Sedgemore, the Labour MP for Hackney South and Shoreditch from 1983 to 2005, spelled out its obituary in the House of Commons: 'The Trowbridge Estate was built amid the naiveté and optimism of the 1960s. Today it embodies the pessimism of the 1980s. It is a monument to misery and insensitivity, which demonstrates only too clearly how that which can be fashionable but which is not rooted in the needs of the people can quickly become a disaster.' In November 2003, the demolition of Rathbone Point and Rachel Point as part of the regeneration of the Nightingale Estate near Hackney Downs brought the number of surviving Hackney tower blocks to less than a hundred.

The Holly Street Estate, which Hackney Council had unsuccessfully proposed in 1973 to extend as far as London Fields by demolishing the Victorian Mapledene Estate, was finally redeveloped in 2003. The new estate still had one tower block, renovated to house the elderly, but the other three had been replaced by low-rise housing, designed by the local practice of Levitt Bernstein Associates in imitation of 'traditional' (i.e. Victorian) London streets. Only one in every ten of the original residents was rehoused in the area and 1,200 properties were offered for private sale as a way of part-subsidising local authority housing provision. Holly Street is now incorporated into the 'Queensbridge Quarter' of sleek, privately-built flats. But problems remain. In 2006 a father of two was knifed to death in Evergreen Square at the centre of the estate, and the 'Holly Street Boys' still engage in sometimes deadly warfare with their nearby arch rivals the 'London Fields Boys'.

The 'right to buy', first proposed on a large scale by Horace Cutler when he was the Conservative leader of the GLC and taken up with enthusiasm by Margaret Thatcher in the Housing Act of 1980, further diminished housing stock available for the less well-off. By 1987 over one million council houses had been sold to their tenants, who paid the market value minus a discount, later reduced, in proportion to the amount they had paid in rent over the years. While there had been an increase in council house occupation between 1971 and 1981 in Hackney, there was a fall of 10% between 1981 and 1991, presumably due to the sale of council houses and the transfer of property to housing associations. The proceeds of these sales went to the local authority, but rather than ploughing the money back into building new houses, the authority was obliged to pay off any debts to the Treasury first. The net effect of the right to buy in Hackney was that it depleted council housing at a faster rate than it was replaced.

Other parts of Hackney were changing at the end of the century too. Owner occupation doubled from just over 9,000 households in 1971 to over 20,000 in 1991. Gentrification arrived in parts of Hackney in the mid-1980s, with properties radically renovated and many multi-occupation houses returned to single-family use. The press was drawing attention to Hackney's 'desirable terraces': Victoria Park, De Beauvoir Town, Lower Clapton and some of the streets around London Fields were particularly popular. 'Within a few moments walk of my gracious Hackney home, I have two excellent public libraries,

The leaning tower of 'Ackney on the Trowbridge Estate, 1985. (Chris Dorley-Brown)

8A

the church I attend and a number of friendly shops .... My house which was indeed in a sad state when I bought it has been put in order by me .... The bomb site opposite has been filled with council houses – not a dreary block but a reasonable imitation of a London town house. I like the street markets, the frenetic activity on Ridley Road, the garden market [presumably Columbia Road] on a Sunday', a satisfied incomer to De Beauvoir Town wrote to *The Times* on 26 August 1983.

A small proportion of this demand has been met by new-build speculative housing, ranging from Sutton Square near St John's Church (1984), a neo-neo-Georgian enclave designed by CZGW for the house-builder Kentish Homes, to the remarkable series of hi-tech blocks of flats that line the Regent's Canal – of which the most striking is perhaps AHMM's Adelaide Wharf (2007) with its array of orange, red and yellow enamel-clad balconies suspended from crane-like cantilevers on the roof. But Hackney's property boom has largely relied on the regeneration of its attractive but dilapidated Georgian and Victorian housing stock, either on the part of enterprising owner-occupiers or by canny landlords with an eye to increased rental or resale value.

Gentrification in turn fuelled a resurgence of interest in the borough's rich but much-abused architectural heritage. The first two-thirds of our period were not kind to the antiquities of Hackney. Many of the best 18th-century houses had been swept away in the inter-war period, including the exceptional 179 Lower Clapton Road, a magnificent Baroque mansion of 1712, finally demolished in 1933 to make way for an early LCC housing block. The Blitz claimed many more casualties, including Smirke's great Greek Revival church at West Hackney. The worst of these losses was Brooke House in Upper Clapton, a late medieval courtyard house once owned by Henry VIII. Damaged by bombing in 1940, it was eventually pulled down in 1955. Meanwhile, the LCC/GLC's Ringway 1 scheme threatened to drive an eight-lane motorway through the middle of Hackney, with giant clover-leaf intersections at Dalston and Hackney Wick.

Local resistance to such schemes crystallised in May 1967 with the formation of the Hackney Society, under its first president, John Betjeman. Its membership was a mixture of early gentrifiers and established residents, united by their willingness to 'find something of great value in the buildings of Hackney ... a priceless heritage which it is impossible to replace'. Early campaigns, like that against the East Cross Route, now the A12 at Hackney Wick, were noble failures, but the Society added its voice to the chorus of opposition that eventually scuppered Ringway 1. It also helped to bring about a revolution in official attitudes to the area's historic residential architecture.

The council's initial policy of rebuilding 95% of its housing stock, including the whole of De Beauvoir Town, gradually shifted to one of retention and

The brightly coloured balconies of Adelaide Wharf on Queensbridge Road. (Tim Soar)

Two incarnations of Broadway Market. *Left,* a photograph taken *c.*1912 of the bustling street.

Right, sixty years later, a sad sight, with few shops remaining open. (Hackney Archives)

adaptation. Hackney's first conservation areas were designated in 1969; there are now 29 such areas, jealously guarded by local advisory committees and by the Society itself. The 'rescue' of the 16th-century Sutton House in Homerton likewise exemplifies this trend. Acquired by the National Trust in 1938, it was let to a succession of tenants and by the mid-'80s had become a squat. The Trust vainly sought to dispose of it, but intense pressure from the 'Save Sutton House' campaign led to its being restored and opened to the public in 1991.

The revival of Broadway Market adjacent to London Fields exemplifies the pleasures – and perils – of gentrification. One of London's oldest chartered markets, on the ancient drovers' road from East Anglia to the slaughterhouses of Smithfield, Broadway Market had by the late 20th century been reduced to a couple of produce stalls and a few small shops, with graffiti defiantly proclaiming: 'Broadway Market is not a Sinking Ship, It's a Submarine'. Commercial salvation came in the form of a farmer's style market which opened in May 2004. A smaller version of the famous Borough Market at London Bridge, it sells continental cheeses, artisanal bread, organic fruit and vegetables – though with a greengrocer's stall that has weathered 50 years of trading still on the same site.

But the revival also brought dissent, epitomising the 'gentrification' debate Hackney has long had with itself. In 1999 the Council, needing to plug a £72 million hole in its finances, informed the shopkeepers of Broadway Market that their shops (and that sometimes included their homes) were to be sold off in 28 days to the highest bidder. In fact, the leaseholders' bids were declined in favour of a developer representing what the council described as 'best value' – and ready cash – though his company paid less in some cases than the leaseholders were prepared to offer. A legal battle ensued: Francesca's Café, one of the properties sold,

was occupied by protestors resisting the bailiffs throughout the winter of 2005, and until 2008 there was a well-supported financial appeal to retain the Nutritious Food Gallery at No. 71 for the existing tenant, Spirit, who had been trading there since 1993. It appears that despite the predilection for a latté and bruschetta society, many newcomers to Hackney also want to preserve the diverse nature of the borough that reflects the varied daily wants and needs of its inhabitants. In addition, Chatsworth Road on the edge of the Lea Valley is now striving to establish itself as Clapton's answer to Broadway Market.

If housing provision changed over the course of the century in Hackney, so did patterns of employment. In the early 1900s, Shoreditch and the southern and eastern parts of Hackney were still very much industrial districts. This was the traditional centre of London's furniture trade, with a honeycomb of small workshops around Hoxton Square and along the railway lines between London Fields and Mare Street. The 18th-century almshouses on Kingsland Road were transformed in 1914 into the Geffrye Museum, intended to showcase this trade. In 1901, there were over 5,000 people working as cabinet makers, joiners and French-polishers, and as late as the 1920s there were still pianos being made in Hackney as well as office equipment.

The inventors of the Put-U-Up sofa bed, Greaves & Thomas, had various workshops in the area including one in Amhurst Road which closed in around 1965. Hardly furniture-makers, but an important part of the Hackney economy, were the pressure die-casters Lesney Products. With a workforce of 1,500 turning out Matchbox toys, they were probably the borough's largest employer when they went into receivership in 1982.

The clothing industry was another staple form of employment. In 1964 there were almost as many

Left, Broadway Market today, with its Saturday market.

Right, Vegetables on a market stall on Ridley Road. (John Hooper)

Simpson's Factory, looking down from Stamford Grove, 1935. (Simpson's Archive)

such enterprises in Hackney as in the traditional heartland in the East End, with some contingent outwork – or sweated labour – for local housewives. Large factories were devoted to men's tailoring. Simpson's, which developed the DAKS clothing brand in 1934, had a model factory in Stoke Newington, employing 2,000 until it closed in *c.*1982 and the premises were taken over as a Turkish community centre. Another model factory was Horne Bros. at Durringo House, King Edward's Road, from 1922 until 1987, soon after which the building was redeveloped for residential use.

The furriers Swears & Wells, Barrymores and their successor Willerby & Co., the men's outfitters and hire company Moss Bros and the East End clothing firm of Alfred Poliakoff all had premises in Hackney for much of the 20th century – as did Burberry's, the traces of which are still present today in its tourist-magnet factory outlet shop in Chatham Place off Morning Lane.

By the 1930s London's footwear industry was centred on Hackney with shoe and boot factories (most, like the clothiers, Jewish-owned) dotted throughout the borough. Cordwainer's Technical College moved to Mare Street in 1946, and was finally incorporated into the London College of Fashion in 2000. Its successful graduates include the shoemakers Jimmy Choo, Patrick Cox and Emma Hope.

On the eve of the Second World War, only five of London's 28 boroughs had more industrial premises than Hackney, whose factories and workshops employed a total of 46,333 workers. The slow leeching away of industry after the Second World War, part of the decentralization of London's industrial base, accelerated dramatically in the 1970s. Clothing manufacturers were particularly hard-hit with competition from small back-street outfits undercutting prices by employing immigrant labour on scandalously low wages. By 1981, male unemployment stood at 16.1%, the second highest rate in London, while average weekly earnings – £133.50 for men, less still for women – were the lowest in the capital.

The industrial exodus brought its own opportunities. The disused workshops and warehouses of Shoreditch/Hoxton were colonised as makeshift artists' studios, and the area became synonymous with the Young British Art scene. By the turn of the millennium, however, any struggling young artists had long since been priced out of the area by the fashionable loft apartments and nightclubs clustering around Jay Jopling's White Cube Gallery. Many moved to units around London Fields, only to be pursued once more by the ruthless economics of gentrification and pushed yet further out, this time to the derelict light-industrial spaces of Hackney Wick.

The arrival of the 2012 Olympic Park has had a great and contentious impact on the Wick, still one of the borough's poorest areas. The chemical and manufacturing industries that once clustered here have nearly all departed, and the premises of the British Oxygen Company, and of Setright Registers – whose patent ticket machine was used by bus companies the world over – have now been taken over by the Olympics Development Authority. The Hackney Wick Greyhound Stadium, which closed in 2003, now houses the 2012 Olympic media and broadcast centre, and after the games will be sold for commercial use. There was a well supported – but unsuccessful – campaign by plot-holders and others to halt the supposedly temporary clearance of the Manor Garden allotments, 80 plots provided by a director of Baring's Bank in 1900 for people without gardens to grow vegetables.

Meanwhile, the Hackney Wick Area Action Plan envisages yet more sweeping changes, based – in the typically breathless booster-speak – on a 'vision' of the Wick as 'a vibrant stimulating place to live, work and visit, with an attractive mix of housing … strong public transport links, safe walking and cycling links, local services and infrastructure, and excellent access to high quality parkland, open space and waterways'.

In fact, Hackney remains a poor borough with multiple social problems. On 26 October 2006, a Channel Four programme identified Hackney as 'the worst place in England' to live, citing the lack of affordable housing, the fact that burglary figures were four times the national average and that Clapton has its very own 'murder mile'. Long-held stereotypes about the borough – Why does the Regent's Canal run through Hackney? So it doesn't get shot! – still seemed to have some purchase.

The fight-back was swift. Hackney's mayor, Jules Pipe, admitted that the borough had its problems, but said that they were those most inner-city areas shared. 'I Love Hackney' cards and mugs were produced for Christmas and sold at Hackney Museum, reviving the pioneering poster campaign mounted by Hackney Society members in 1967. An article appeared in the *Guardian*, written by a resident celebrating Hackney's vitality and diversity, without denying that 'some things about it are crap'.

The 'crap' includes the still-high rate of crime. The notorious murder of Jack 'The Hat' McVitie by Reggie Kray took place in Evering Road, Stoke Newington in 1967, and for decades Sandringham Road off Kingsland Road was on the front line of crack cocaine dealing.

In 2003 alone the police claimed to have closed down 200 Hackney 'crack houses', and the borough is one of the top five in London for gun crime. Furthermore, there has been a long history of troubled relations between the police and some young black members of the community. 'Operation Jackpot' was an investigation into corruption in the Stoke Newington police force. It reported in 1994 that two officers were suspended, an outcome that the Hackney Community Defence Association condemned as a 'whitewash'. The incidence of burglary in Hackney is about twice the national average, as are thefts of and from vehicles and violence against the person, while robbery is eight times more common in Hackney than in the nation at large. However, the recent trend has been more encouraging: crime rates are estimated to have fallen by 39.5% between 2004 and 2009.

What about education? Does that fall under the heading of what is 'crap' about Hackney? In the early years of the 20th century Hackney's schoolchildren were better served than most. In 1903, when the LCC took over the functions of the London School Board, there were 28 elementary schools in the Metropolitan Borough, with accommodation for 33,758. Several had classes for children continuing their education beyond elementary level, with Cassland Road School being entirely higher grade. In addition, there were seven special schools for disabled children, and 18 other schools received education grants. By 1909 the Grocers' Company School had been transferred into the state system; renamed as Hackney Downs School, it produced a long list of distinguished alumni including the playwrights Harold Pinter and Stephen Berkoff, the kidney transplant pioneer Ralph Shackleton, the washing machine entrepreneur John Bloom (whose motto was 'it's no sin to make a profit') and four current members of the House of Lords.

Among London's first purpose-built comprehensives was Woodberry Down School (1950-55), the centrepiece of the estate of the same name. In the early days it was a showcase establishment, and in the 1970s the headmaster was the well-known progressive educationalist Michael Marland. But structural problems beset the concrete-framed building, and the school closed in 1981. Hackney still boasts three outstanding school buildings of the late 20th century: Haggerston School for Girls (1962-7), a bold exercise in Corbusian geometry by Ernö Goldfinger; the GLC's Benthal Infant School in Stoke Newington (1966-7), with its tent-roofed classrooms and child-friendly honeycomb layout; and Ickburgh School in Clapton (1972), a special school built for the Spastics Society to an early design by Foster & Partners.

By the end of the century, however, while many Hackney primary schools were receiving 'good' or 'outstanding' Oftsted reports, the borough's secondary schools had – with a few exceptions – become a disaster zone, combining low educational standards with absenteeism and unruly, often violent behaviour. In 2002, only 31% of Hackney students gained five or more GCSEs at grades A* to C, compared to 53% nationally. In that year, the Education Secretary dissolved the Hackney LEA and handed over its responsibilities to the Learning Trust, a non-profit company chaired by the educationalist Sir Mike Tomlinson.

Meanwhile, a new type of school began to emerge. The Learning and Skills Act 2000 made provision for 'city academies', self-governing foundation schools directly funded by central government but backed by a sponsor who, in return for their 10% stake, would be able to influence the school's curriculum and ethos. On the site of the old Hackney Downs School, one of the first to be shut down under the school-closure programme after long years of gradual decline, the Mossbourne Academy emerged in 2004 as the first phoenix of this new educational philosophy. Sponsored by the transport millionaire Sir Clive Bourne, the buildings

Woodberry Down School, with the woodwork block in the foreground, *c.*1955. (City of London, London Metropolitan Archives)

The entrance hall of Haggerston School for Girls. (Dennis Gilbert)

were designed by Rogers Stirk Harbour as a huge V-plan groundscraper built of laminated timber, symbolically opening its arms to Hackney Downs.

A strictly regulated, very generously funded institution with over 1,000 pupils, its success was noteworthy under its first headmaster Sir Michael Wilshaw, who was appointed head of Ofsted in 2011. 43% of pupils receive free school meals (an index of poverty) while 38% do not have English as a first language. Despite this, exam results topped the national league tables, 87% of children gained A* to C in their GCSE exams, and 10 students were offered Oxbridge places in 2011.

Other new academy schools followed: the Bridge Academy in Haggerston; the Petchey Academy in Dalston; and the City Academy in Homerton. In addition, Hackney has been awarded £170 million by the government, to improve and update all other secondary and special-needs schools in the borough by 2014.

From the days when it was an edge-of-London village to its present incarnation as an inner-city borough, Hackney has had a continuous history of immigrant settlement. The Jewish community, first established in the 18th century, changed markedly at the beginning of the 20th. Rich families had moved out, making way for large numbers of immigrants, most coming from Russia, Poland and parts of central Europe, their numbers swollen in the 1930s by those fleeing Nazi persecution in Germany and Austria. By 1938 there were some 50,00 Jews in north London; a large number were drawn to Stamford Hill, though the area around Well Street had a sizeable population supporting a number of Jewish shops, among the best known being the bakers, B. Smulevitch. In 1915 the magnificent New Synagogue opened in Egerton Road, a very visible sign that Upper Clapton was becoming a more important area for Jews than their traditional home in the East End.

By the 1950s it was claimed that Hackney had the densest concentration of Jews in the country – the Woodberry Down estate had a high proportion, and there were a large number of working-class Jews living in estates around Amhurst Road, while 50% of the pupils at Hackney Downs School were Jewish. However, the Jewish population had changed considerably since the New Synagogue was built. In 1926 the Union of Orthodox Hebrew Congregations, most of whose constituents were affiliated to the Adath Yisroel Synagogue in Stoke Newington, had been established in Stamford Hill, and by the mid 1970s there were some 2,500 Hasidic Jews in the area, including the ultra-orthodox Haredi Jews. These had little connection with the older synagogues, preferring to worship in conventicles, either *shtiebels* (little domestic rooms) or *beth hamedrash* (houses of study) within Stamford Hill's 'square mile of piety'.

The 2001 census revealed that the population of Hasidic Jews in Hackney had risen to around 20,000, the vast majority living in Stamford Hill. As Hasidic Jews are encouraged to have large families – eight or nine is not unknown – the population is calculated to be growing at the rate of 5% a year. An infrastructure of kosher supermarkets, butchers, fishmongers and bakers enable the community to obey the dictates of the Torah and keep apart from non-Jewish culture. The men wear long coats, high black hats or flatter beaver ones depending on the community to which they belong, with ringlets protruding, while the women wear concealing clothes, married women covering their heads with a wig and often also a scarf or hat to protect their modesty on the teeming streets of Stamford Hill.

The children of Stamford Hill's orthodox Jews (a somewhat umbrella term to cover a number of overlapping groups) are educated in one of the area's 32 strictly segregated faith schools. These are privately – and community – funded, though one, the Yesodey Hatorah Senior School for girls in Egerton Road, was granted voluntary-aided status and moved into what Ofsted described as 'superb' new premises in 2005. Its educational standards are also regarded as outstanding by Ofsted, though its principal, Rabbi Abraham Pinter, explained in February 2011 that despite high achievements at A level, his pupils would not go on to university where they would be exposed to such 'evil temptations' as the cinema, television and the internet. Their destiny is to have a family: most have arranged marriages and marry young.

Mossbourne Community Academy. (David Churchill)

The concentration on study of the Torah and Talmudic law rather than secular academic or vocational courses can disadvantage Orthodox Jews in the employment market, and this – along with large family sizes – has ensured that there are high levels of poverty and overcrowding in Stamford Hill. The community network of voluntary agencies helps where it can, and there are some very successful businessmen living in the area, but 70% of the families are in receipt of child benefits, and the perceived reluctance of the Hackney planning department to sanction large loft conversions is seen not to help the problem of overcrowded homes.

The 1948 Nationality Act granted British nationality to all citizens of its current and former colonies, giving them the right to a British passport and to lifelong residency in the UK – an invitation proffered largely in response to the contemporary labour shortage, particularly in medical services and the transport and catering industries. On 22 June 1948, 492 Jamaicans arrived at Tilbury on the former troopship *SS Windrush*, and ten years later around 125,000 African-Caribbeans were living in the UK – many of them settling in London. A graphic illustration of Hackney's shifting ethnic make-up was the fact that by the mid-1970s African-Caribbean boys had largely replaced Jews at Hackney Downs School.

Other ethnic groups followed. After Brent and Harringey, Hackney has London's highest percentage of heads of household from the so-called 'New Commonwealth' and Pakistan, living mainly in the area from Lea Bridge to the south of Stoke Newington and in central Hackney. A report for the North London Muslim Housing Association in 2001 calculated that, out of a total population of 196,904, Muslim groups of all ethnic origins constituted 46,000; 40% of this total were Kurdish or Turkish, 16% Bangladeshi, 14% Indian, 10% Pakistani, 10% Somalian or Eritrean and 10% of other origin.

In May 1978 Hackney was chosen by the Commission for Racial Equality (CRE) as 'a suitable and representative borough on which to concentrate a comprehensive investigation of the causes of … discrimination and disadvantage' in the public housing sector. The interim conclusion reached four years later was that Hackney had 'unlawfully discriminated against various persons of West Indian, Asian or African origin' ('black people' in the terminology of the report), 'who were rehoused from the Council's waiting list, rehoused as homeless cases, or rehoused as a result of being decanted from their existing accommodation'. In effect, the housing offered to black people was not of a 'like quality to that afforded to white persons in similar need of housing'. A larger proportion of white applicants were offered accommodation in newly-built houses and estates, whereas black people were more likely to find themselves in run-down, inter-war estates such as Hindle, Wigan, Shacklewell and Nisbet.

Hackney Council's response to these findings was 'constructive and positive' according to the CRE. The chairman of the Housing Committee, Councillor Charles Clarke, who would later serve as Labour Home Secretary, accepted the report fully, agreed to implement its recommendations and to 'support to the very fullest extent the effort of the CRE in seeking to stamp out racial discrimination' in the allocation of municipal housing. Training programmes were initiated, a senior post was created to monitor progress and a committee comprising representatives of tenants and various ethnic groups was set up.

The ethnic diversity of Hackney is a vibrant presence in numerous ways. There are 17 mosques in the borough, one of the most recent being the Suleymaniye Mosque on Kingsland Road, first established in a small flat above a supermarket in the 1980s and reopened in 1999 as a splendid six-storey building clad in patterned tilework with a golden dome and towering minaret; it is the headquarters of the UK Turkish Islamic Cultural Centre. Shops, restaurants and cafés throw back clear cultural reflections too. Kosher butchers, bakers and supermarkets cluster mainly around Stamford Hill; there is a trail of Vietnamese restaurants along Mare Street and Kingsland Road, while in Stoke Newington Turkish kebab houses and Ocakbasi restaurants predominate. Gastropubs, that infallible index of gentrification, are opening over the borough from Stoke Newington Church Street to the residential roads around London Fields and Broadway Market. Cooke's Eel and Pie shop in Broadway Market still serves the traditional Cockney dish, as does the Hoxton shop which opened in 1910. Caribbean food is sold in shops across the borough and at the daily market at Ridley Road, one of Hackney's busiest markets with dozens of food and clothes stalls, surrounded by Halal butchers and a 24-hour bagel shop.

The long-planned 'cultural quarter' centred round Hackney's monumental Town Hall and square in Mare Street is slowly coming to fruition. The neoclassical Town Hall was built in 1934-7 by the architects Lanchester and Lodge, its chaste white shell of Portland stone concealing an opulent 'cruise liner' interior. To the north is the Hackney Empire, Frank Matcham's phantasmagorical variety palace of stucco and terracotta: opened in 1901, it was rescued in 1986 from an ignominious existence as a bingo hall and TV studio, and finally restored and extended by Tim Ronalds Architects in 2004.

Opposite the Town Hall is the former Methodist Central Hall of 1925, briefly used as a nightclub before its recent reinvention as the Hackney Picturehouse, a four-screen cinema and gallery which complements the magnificent 1930s Art Deco cinema, the Rio, in Kingsland Road. Hackney's new central library and museum make up the fourth side of the square, part of a Chicagoesque complex of glass and steel buildings by Hodder & Partners that also includes the main council offices.

Left, The new Town Hall in Hackney, almost complete, with the last remnant of the old, 1937.

Right, Detail of the 2004 extension to the Hackney Empire by TIm Ronalds Architiects. (Grant Smith)

The tentacles of culture stretch beyond the official 'quarter'. The Carnegie Library in Homerton has been transformed into Chats Palace, an arts and community space, while the Vortex jazz club relocated from Stoke Newington to the 'Dalston Culture House' in Gillett Square off Kingsland High Street. Across the road is the new site of the Arcola Theatre, a two-theatre space housed in a former paint factory. It prides itself on the innovative range of its productions, sometimes with a local edge, such as the powerful *Come out Eli*, a play about the longest police siege in British history which started on a bitterly cold Boxing Day in 2002 in Graham Road and ended 16 days later with the death of the gunman Eli Hall.

One cultural venue that has been lost is the Four Aces Club, started in 1966 by the Jamaican Newton Dunbar in the old Dalston Theatre building on Dalston Lane. For the next 30 years the Four Aces mapped the music scene, drawing visitors such as Bob Marley and Bob Dylan to its mix of soul and reggae in the early years when Jimmy Cliff and Desmond Dekker, 'reggae's first super star', played there. But, as Dunbar sadly says, 'you can hold four aces as a hand and still lose'. In 2007 the building was demolished to make way for the 'retail-led regeneration' of Dalston Cross – a development of shops, bars and high-rise luxury apartments around the new London Overground station – despite resistance from many local residents disquieted to see what they regarded as the rubbing out of Hackney's cultural heritage.

In 1987 Diane Abbott became Britain's first black female MP when she was elected for Hackney North and Stoke Newington, a seat she still holds in 2012. Hackney was declared a 'nuclear-free zone' in 1985, a fact recorded in the exuberant mural in Dalston Lane painted by Ray Walker, and completed by his wife Anne after his premature death, to celebrate the 'Peace Carnival' held in the borough the previous year. But it was not until 2012 that this policy was given practical effect when the coming of the Olympics led to a ban on the transport of nuclear waste through Dalston Junction.

Hackney and its environs have long been home to radical politics – of both right and left. The tradition begun by Richard Price, Mary Wollstonecraft and Anna Laetitia Barbauld at Newington Green Unitarian Church continued in 2008 when the church became the first religious establishment in Britain to refuse to conduct marriage services until all couples have equal marriage rights. This earned it the predictable tabloid soubriquet, 'the gay rights church'. On the railings a banner was able to proclaim '300 years of dissent'. In the 1960s members of the anarchist 'Angry Brigade' were holed up in Amhurst Road, while the artist Helen Chadwick and the musician Genesis P. Orridge were among those who occupied a terrace of condemned houses in Beck Road, off Mare Street, before the council relented and allowed the squatters to rent the properties.

At the other end of the radical political spectrum was the British Union of Fascists. In the 1930s Oswald Mosley moved his 'Black House' HQ from Chelsea to the Balls Pond Road and spewed anti-Semitic propaganda to crowds gathered in Ridley Road market, the site of frequent and often violent clashes between the Blackshirt 'biff boys' and anti-fascist protestors.

Astonishingly, in the immediate post-war years fascism revived, and in 1947 Ridley Road was again the location for violent clashes between Mosley's supporters and the anti-fascists. The latter were led by the '43 Group' of Jewish war veterans founded by Morris Beckman, which adopted the yellow star as its emblem. These confrontations drew crowds of up to 3,000, and there were accusations that the police sided with the fascists, allowing them to carry on with their anti-Semitic, anti-black inflammatory speeches despite much strong local opposition.

Beckman's group disbanded in 1950, confident that the fascist threat had passed, but by the 1970s the hard-right National Front was attracting considerable support. They met their match in the equally vociferous Anti-Nazi League which held a Rock Against Racism concert headlined by The Clash

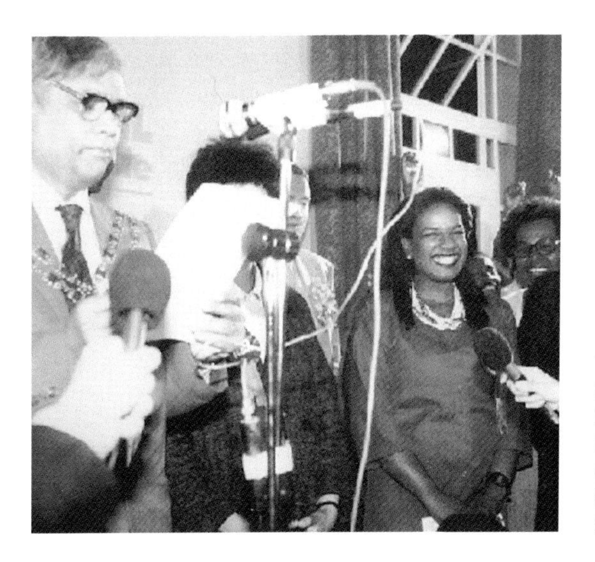

The declaration of Diane Abbott as the Member for Hackney North, the first black woman to sit in the Commons, 1987. (Hackney Archives)

in Victoria Park on 30 April 1978. Later that year, 19-year-old Michael Ferreira was knifed by three white youths shouting National Front slogans. The British National Party (BNP), a breakaway group from the NF, was founded in 1982 and continued its activities in Hackney into the 1990s, though its main London stronghold was further east in Tower Hamlets and Newham.

Hackney's transport – and its inadequacies – has been a source of fascination and frustration throughout the last century. In the 1920s there were still horse-drawn carts on the cobbled streets of Hackney, and drinking troughs on every main thoroughfare. The coming of motorised transport did not displace the use of draft horses, and 'the sweet smell of their sweat mingled with the odour of petrol fumes', according to Alan Wilson who grew up in Hackney in the inter-war years. Some carts carried coal, the horses driven by men with dust-blackened faces wearing black aprons and hoods to protect them as they humped the sacks of coal, shouting their wares, '1s 11d a hundredweight'. Brewers' drays pulled by huge carthorses transported barrels of beer, which were rolled down a ladder to the pavement outside a public house, and then via a manhole or trap door into the pub cellar.

Mick Clark of the British Union of Fascists addressing a rally in Dalston, *c.*1945. (David Renton)

The milk cart was smaller, carrying metal churns banded with brass hoops. In the 19th century such churns had a tap and the milkman carried a measure to dispense milk to housewives who queued up with a jug, but before the First World War this somewhat insanitary habit had been abandoned, and milk was delivered in bottles. Alan Wilson remembers being perplexed when in the late 1930s he was asked to write a school essay on why a horse was better than a motor van for delivering milk. Recalling deliveries outside his home near Victoria Park, he ventured to suggest that 'the horse was better at starting and stopping than a petrol engine. That while the milkman was delivering the milk, a well-trained horse would move onto the next door.'

By the 1950s, milkmen's horses had given way to the battery-driven milk float, and in recent years even these have become an increasingly rare sight in Hackney streets as corner shops, many owned by recent immigrants to Britain and prepared to stay open as late as any Victorian shop, sell milk in plastic bottles almost around the clock.

Horses were also seen on the streets of Hackney conveying rag-and-bone men, who might reward children for the donation of scrap metal or some other commodity with sweets or a goldfish. And no funeral of any standing would be complete without a horse-drawn hearse, the horses arrayed with fine feather plumes on their heads and reins hung with highly polished brass. This is a sight still occasionally to be seen at Hackney funerals.

But there were more modern forms of transport too. Horse-drawn trams had first come to Hackney in 1872 with a line from Moorgate to Stamford Hill along Kingsland and Stoke Newington Roads. This intersected at Dalston with an east-west route running from Aldersgate to Islington. The network was extended over the course of the next decades, and electrification began in 1907, so that by the outbreak of war in 1914 the system was almost complete. Additions during the 1920s included a line across Victoria Park from Bethnal Green to South Hackney and a service along Amhurst Road linking Hackney and Clapton with Finsbury Park and Camden Town.

Motor buses supplemented the tram network from the early 1900s. Alan Wilson remembered the buses of his childhood well.' They carried history with them. The conductor still spoke of "inside" instead of "downstairs" and "outside" instead of "upstairs". They were strange vehicles. At the rear was a curling open staircase apparently stuck on as an afterthought. It resembled a fire escape. Climbing that staircase on a wet and windy day was an unpleasant experience.' The upper deck, where second-class passengers sat, was open to the elements, and was only finally roofed over in the late 1930s.

The London Passenger Transport Board took over all the privately-run bus and tram routes in 1933, converting the latter to trolley-buses in 1939; the last of these were finally phased out in 1962. Public ownership was maintained under London Transport, the LPTB's successor body, but in 1990 the private sector moved back into transport provision when the Kentish Bus Company was awarded three of the nine routes put out to tender by the borough.

Hackney was one of the first places in London to experiment with articulated 'bendy buses', which in 2002 replaced the familiar double-decker Routemasters on routes such as the 38 and 73. Popular with the disabled and parents with buggies, and also with fare dodgers, they were less so with cyclists and the Mayor of London, Boris Johnson, who began phasing them out shortly after taking office in 2008.

Hackney has always suffered from not being part of the London underground system, but for many years the north-south overground lines from

Lawrence Gowing's painting of Mare Street, 1937. (Courtesy of the Shrewsbury College of Arts & Technology)

Dalston Junction to Broad Street and from Enfield to Liverpool Street via Hackney Downs carried thousands of commuters daily. Three hundred trains a day stopped at Broad Street in 1903. North of Dalston Junction the Broad Street line forked to join the main crosstown route of the North London Railway, which provided a secondary east-west axis. However, passenger traffic on the eastern arm towards Poplar and the Docks ceased during the Second World War, and Broad Street itself gradually withered and died in the post-war years, finally closing in 1986.

Hackney's transport isolation was somewhat ameliorated in 1980 when the old NLR route was revived as the North London Link Line, with funding from the GLC, and five years later the entire line was reopened for electric trains running from North

Woolwich to Richmond via Hackney Wick, Homerton, Hackney Central and Dalston Kingsland. This service, run by the Silverlink franchise from 1994, was taken over by Transport for London (TFL) in 2007 as part of what it now designates as the London Overground. Dalston Junction, closed along with Broad Street in 1986, was revived in 2010 as part of the extended Overground service from Highbury to New Cross and West Croydon. However, the promise of a connection to the Crossrail route, originally mooted in the Abercrombie Plan in 1944, still remains unfulfilled in 2012.

Nearly 7% of Hackney's population regularly cycle to work – the highest proportion of any London borough – and the number is growing every year according to census figures. This accounts for the growing number of cycle retail and repair shops in the borough, and the active campaign on the part of Hackney Cyclists and others to extend cycle lanes and restrict the number of one-way streets and other urban hazards. The dangers of cycling remain, made all too evident by the tragic appearance of white 'memorial bikes'.

But cycling isn't all about getting to work or couriers on bikes outpacing the Post Office or even concern for the environment. It is a leisure activity too. Cyclists use the towpaths along the Grand Union and Regent's Canals, and speed through Victoria Park and London Fields – where the Lido, built in 1931, reopened in 2006 as a 50-metre Olympic standard heated pool following a strenuous 18-year campaign. But the greatest of this inner-city borough's green 'lungs' is the Lee Valley, a gradually narrowing wedge of countryside that follows the course of the Lea from Hertford to Stratford and Canning Town. It includes the vast expanse of Hackney Marshes, which at one time incorporated 128 football pitches where luminaries such as David Beckham honed their skills, and which still re-echo to the sound of young footballers cursing their team mates and referees.

Plans for a Lee Valley Regional Park, intended to bring the countryside of Essex and Hertfordshire to the slums of East London, formed part of the Abercrombie Plan – a visionary example of 'constructive, preservative and regenerative planning'. In the 1960s Hackney's mayor, Lou Sherman, persuaded other London and Hertfordshire and Essex local authorities to share this vision for the 'challenge of leisure' – and to help foot the bill.

The Civic Trust drew up a blueprint for the regeneration of the valley, embracing outdoor leisure and indoor arts to 'rival the Tivoli Gardens in Copenhagen'. The proposals included aviaries, exotic oriental gardens and a 'Fun Palace' of scaffolding, gantries, stages and installations, designed by the visionary architect Cedric Price and promoted by Joan Littlewood of the Theatre Royal Stratford. The Lee Valley Regional Park Act came into law on 1 January 1967, envisaging an entirely transformed Lee Valley within 15 years – or less.

It did not happen. In the words of Laurie Elks, a joint founder of the Lee Valley Association, the 1980s ushered in 'an era of pragmatism' and it became increasingly clear that most of the grandiloquent schemes for the area simply could not or would not be funded in the ways that had been anticipated. In future the concentration would be on regenerating the landscape – turning the disused Middlesex filter beds into a nature reserve is one example of this – and opening up more of the Lee Valley to the public. Nevertheless, the Lee Valley Park Authority, which is supported by ratepayers across the whole of London, Hertfordshire and Essex, continued to feel a 'developmentalist urge', the fruits of which include the ice centre at Lea Bridge and, further afield, the Lee Valley Athletics Centre in Edmonton, both partly funded by national sporting bodies.

The 2012 Olympics changed the mix yet again. Although it had little input into the plans, the Park Authority owns much of the land on which the Olympic site is built and its current Park Development Framework commits it to work in partnership with the Olympics Development Authority to achieve 'a high quality and regionally unique visitor destination' – indeed 'a world class destination combining the best of open space, conservation and sporting excellence'. Hackney holds its breath as much with apprehension as expectation!

* * *

'Lively, diverse, intense cities contain the seeds of their own regeneration', wrote Jane Jacobs in her hugely influential book *The Death and Life of Great American Cities*, first published in 1961. Hackney is a microcosm of that process, with its restless experimentation in housing and education, its ambivalence about what exactly an urban heritage should be, its concern with community needs in a multicultural, economically polarised society, and its desire to provide a safer – and a more sustainable – environment for its inhabitants. Yet, as Jacobs wrote in the same book, 'cities have the capability of providing something for everybody, only because, and only when, they are created by everybody'. Hackney still seems to defy the ominous-sounding current suggestion for 'managed decline' in post-industrial urban spaces and frequently proves itself capable of vibrant, if still very limited, regeneration, renewal and a certain optimism. But Jacobs' remark may serve as a cautionary injunction as this still-troubled, polarised and unequal inner-city borough enters its Olympic year.

The Olympic Park, looking over the roofs of Hackney Wick, from the tower of St Mary of Eton Church. (Grant Smith)

Notes for Further Reading

1612

Details of parish records can be found in the Hackney Archives and London Metropolitan Archives. Other sources of information are *The Victoria County History*, Vol. X, for Hackney Parish, published for the Institute of Historical Research by Oxford University Press, 1995, www.victoriacountyhistory.ac.uk; and *Survey of London*, Vol. 8, for St Leonard's Shoreditch, published by Batsford for the LCC, 1922. For a picture of Shoreditch in the late 16th century, see Charles Nicholl, *The Lodger: Shakespeare on Silver Street*, Allen Lane, 2007, and John Marriott, *Beyond the Tower: A History of East London*, Yale University Press, 2011.

The most detailed published account of Sutton House is *A Tudor Courtier's House in Hackney*, by Victor Belcher, Richard Bond, Mike Gray and Andy Wittrick, published by English Heritage in association with the National Trust, 2004. Hugh Trevor-Roper's entry in the *Dictionary of National Biography*, 2004, provides background to Thomas Sutton.

For Matthias L'Obel, John Gerard and Edward Zouche, see Margaret Willes, *The Making of the English Gardener*, Yale University Press, 2011. For Tudor market gardens and the feeding of the City, see Malcolm Thick's *The Neat House Gardens: Early Market Gardening around London*, Prospect Books, 1998.

Christopher Whitfield provides an account of the Olimpicks in *Robert Dover and the Cotswold Games: Annalia Dubrensia*, distributed by Henry Sotheran, 1962.

1712

England's pre-publication censorship laws expired in 1695, producing the world's first free press. This chapter has mined newspaper reports for reports and narratives. Early newspapers are unbeatable primary sources for the Hackney historian, chronicling life, misdemeanours, crime, spectacles and commerce, in a rich and entertaining fashion. An abundance of London's daily, bi-weekly, tri-weekly and weekly London newspapers have been digitized by Gale, and are most easily accessible in the British Library.

Diaries show us the world of Hackney from various personal viewpoints. The most faithful, complete edition of Pepys' diary was edited by Robert Latham and William Matthews, and first published by Bell & Hyman in 1983. Daniel Defoe's *A Tour Through the Whole Island of Great Britain*, 1722, captures the essence of the Hackney villages *en passant*. For a frank and highly entertaining portrait of life in early 18th-century Hackney, see the voluminous diary of law student Dudley Ryder. A heavily truncated edition of this was published in 1939 by William Matthews, as *The Diary of Dudley Ryder*. The original short-hand version and printed transcript resides in the archive department of the magnificent Sandon Hall in Staffordshire.

A valuable dimension to any primary Hackney research can be gleaned from excellent 18th-century maps. Most famous is John Rocques's *Map of the Parish of Hackney c.1746*, although sections of Hoxton and Shoreditch are visible on his classic map of London, Westminster, and Southwark. More elegant and detailed, perhaps, is Peter Chassereau's *Survey of Shoreditch*, 1745.

The secondary reading on 18th-century Hackney is diverse and wide-ranging; the survey undertaken for this chapter was inspired by curiosity and caprice rather than a desire to undertake a comprehensive study of every possible source. In his Victorian study *The History and Antiquities of the Parish of Hackney*, topographer William Robinson undertook to 'trace ancient structures now no more, and other which are magnificent even in decay'. His meticulous, beautifully illustrated study is most noteworthy for its contribution to the architectural history of Hackney, but it lacks a human face. Elizabeth Robinson's *Lost Hackney*, 1989, is an engaging study along similar lines. The best overview of the social, economic, cultural, intellectual and topographic history of Hackney remains *The Victoria County History*, Vol.X (see 1612 above).

Beyond this, the historiography is fragmented, with many historians filtering Hackney's rich history through the prism of their own research interests. The best starting point is to punch the keyword 'Hackney' into the Institute of Historical Research's online *Bibliography of British and Irish History*, specifying an 18th-century timespan. This is most easily accessed via the British Library terminals; it produces a wealth of articles, many of them from the journal *Hackney History*. Of these works, the chapter draws upon in particular: Tony Coomb's illustrated book *'Tis a Mad World at Hogsdon*, published in 1975 (the title from an early broadside ballad); 'The Mad-house Keepers of Hackney' in *Hackney History*, Vol. 8; 'Dick Turpin in Hackney'; Emma Acosta's enlightening article 'Spaces of Dissent and the Public Sphere in Hackney, Stoke Newington, and Newington Green' in *Eighteenth-century Life*, Vol. 27, 2003; 'Restoration Hackney: Haven for the Ejected?'.

Finally, the section on Hackney coffee-houses draws upon Matthew Green's own research – in particular his DPhil thesis 'Londoners and the News: Responses to the Political Press, 1695 to 1742' and *The Lost World of the London Coffeehouse*, to be published by Bracketpress through the Idler Academy later in 2012.

1812

The primary archival sources consulted were located in Hackney Archives and London Metropolitan Archives. Information about early 19th-century Hackney can also be found in the online records of the Old Bailey, www.oldbaileyonline.org, and also in *The Times* digital archive from 1785. This study also utilised Ann Robey's original research undertaken for numerous LB Hackney Conservation Area Appraisals – all can be found online at www.hackney.gov.uk. An important secondary source was *The Victoria County History*, Vol. X (see 1612 above for details). Contemporary accounts consulted included John Middleton's *View of the Agriculture of Middlesex*, 1798, and Daniel Lysons' *The Environs of London*, 1811.

For further information about Benjamin Walsh and Pond House, see Ann Robey, 'A Scoundrel and a Scandal: Benjamin Walsh and Pond House', *Hackney History*, 2010. On the subject of gardening in Hackney, further fascinating detail can be found in David Solman's *Loddiges of Hackney: the largest hothouse in the world*, Hackney Society, 1995, and in John Harvey, *Early Nurserymen*, 1974.

Anna Barbauld's poem *Eighteen Hundred and Eleven* can be read online at Project Gutenberg, www.gutenberg.org.

1912

The primary archival sources can be found in Hackney Archives, the Women's Library and London Metropolitan Archives. Other sources of information are from *The Victoria County History*, Vol. X, for Hackney parish, and Vol. VIII, for Islington and Stoke Newington parishes (see 1612 above for details). Information about early 20th-century Hackney can also be found online at *The Times Digital Archive from 1785* and in old editions of *The Kingsland and Hackney Gazette*.

Contemporary accounts include George Dangerfield's *The Strange Death of Liberal England*, Capricorn Books, 1935, and J.L. and Barbara Hammond's *The Village Labourer 1760-1832*, Longmans, 1911.

On the subject of Anglo-Jewry, further information can be found in Michael Bernstein's *Stamford Hill and the Jews before 1915*, 1976, and Sharman Kadish's *The Synagogues of Britain and Ireland: An Architectural and Social History*, Yale University Press 2011. On the subject of the Old Nichol slum, a detailed history can be found in Sarah Wise's *The Blackest Streets: The life and death of a Victorian Slum*, Bodley Head, 2008, and for a more literary account, Arthur Morrison's novel *A Child of the Jago*, Methuen, 1896.

On the subject of suffrage in Hackney, further details can be found in Julia Lafferty's article 'Elizabeth and Mark Wilks: Campaigners for women's suffrage', *Hackney History*, 2009.

Kenneth Morgan, David Jeremy and A.J.A Morris' entries in the *Oxford Dictionary of National Biography*, 2004, provide background to Christopher Addison, Sir Albert Spicer and Horatio Bottomley.

For further information on the Mothers' Hospital and the Salvation Army, see Ken Worpole's 'The Mothers' Hospital', *Hackney – Modern, Restored, Forgotten, Ignored*, Hackney Society, 2009, and http://health.hackneysociety.org

For further information on the Eton Manor Boys' Club, see Ann Robey's 'Eton Manor Boys' Club', *Hackney – Modern, Restored, Forgotten, Ignored.* Primary source material can be found in the Bishopsgate Institute.

2012

For an overall history of Hackney in the 20th century, see David Mander, *A Hackney Century, 1900-1999*, Sutton Publishing, 1999; and *Late Extra: Hackney in the News*, London Borough of Hackney/Sutton Publishing, 2000. For more 'literary' accounts: Iain Sinclair, *Hackney, That Rose-Red Empire: A Confidential Report*, Hamish Hamilton, 2009, and *Ghost Milk: Calling Time on the Grand Project*, Hamish Hamilton, 2011; and Patrick Wright, *A Journey Through Ruins*, Radius, 1991.

There is a long list of sources for Hackney's architecture.

First, books: Ken Allinson's *London Contemporary Architecture*, 5th ed. Architectural Press, 2009; David Batchelder et al, *From Tower to Tower Block*, Hackney Society, 1979; *Buildings at Risk in Hackney*, Hackney Society, 1987; Nicholas Bullock, *Building the Post-War World*, Routledge, 2002; Chris Dorley-Brown, 'Trowbridge Estate' in Lisa Rigg (ed.), *Hackney. Modern, Restored, Forgotten, Ignored*, Hackney Society, 2009; J.H. Forshaw and Patick Abercombie, *County of London Plan*, Macmillan, 1943; Greater London Council, *Home Sweet Home: Housing Designed by the London County Council and Greater London Council Architects*, Academy Editions, 1976; LCC, *A Survey of the Post-War Housing of the London County Council 1945-1949*, LCC, 1949; Miles Glendinning and Stefan Muthesius, *Tower Block: Modern Public Housing in England, Scotland, Wales and Northern Ireland*, Yale University Press; S.P.B Mais, *50 Years of LCC*, Cambridge University Press, 1939; Nikolaus Pevsner and Bridget Cherry, *The Buildings of England: London 4: North*, Yale University Press edition, 2002; Hugh Quigley and Ismay Goldie, *Housing and Slum Clearance in London*, Methuen, 1934; Elizabeth Robinson, *Lost Hackney*, Hackney Society, 1989, and *Twentieth-Century Buildings in Hackney*, Hackney Society, 1999; and Isobel Watson, *Hackney and Stoke Newington Past*, Historical Publications, 2nd ed.

Articles: *Architectural Design, October 1967*; *Architect's Journal,* 27 October 1949, 13 November 1985, 17 May 1990; *Architectural Review,* September 1949; *Builder,* 20 July 1945; *Building,* 29 March 1974; Peter Foynes, 'The Rise of the High Rise: Post-War Housing in Hackney', *Hackney History*, Vol.1, 1995; Simon Parker, 'From the Slums to the Suburbs: Labour Party Policy, the LCC, and the Woodberry Down Estate, Stoke Newington, 1934-1961, *London Journal*, 24:2, 1999; Stefan Muthesius, '"It is as though we start a new life": Council Housing in Shoreditch, 1945-50', *Hackney History*, Vol. 13, 2007; Isobel Watson, 'The first generation of flats', *Hackney History,* Vol. 11, 2005.

For the Jewish community: Mick Brown, 'Inside the World of London's Ultra-Orthodox Jews', *Daily Telegraph*, 25 February 2011; *Jews in an Inner London Borough (Hackney)*, Research Unit, the Board of Deputies of British Jews, not dated but *c.*1972.

For Hackney's experiences in the World War II: Jennifer Golden, *Hackney at War*, Alan Sutton Publishing, 1995; *London County Council Bomb Damage Maps, 1939-1945*, Ann Saunders (ed.), London Topographical Society, 2005.

On Hackney's social issues: Liz Bisset and Alan Harding/Low Pay Unit, *Poor Hackney!*, Hackney Borough Council, 1983; William Bradley, 'The gentrification of Broadway Market', *Hackney History*, Vol. 16, 2010; Tim Bulter, '"People Like Us": The gentrification of Hackney in the 1980s', in Tim Butler and Michael Rustin (eds); *Rising in the East: The Regeneration of London,* Lawrence & Wishart, 1996; *Gentrification and the Middle Classes*, Ashgate, 1997; Butt Riazat, 'Is Hackney really the worst place to live?', *Guardian,* 26 October 2006; *The New Survey of London Life & Labour*, Vol. III, VI & IX, P.S. King, 1932-5; *Race and Council Housing in Hackney*, Commission for Racial Equality, 1984; Hari Kunzru, 'Market Forces', *Guardian,* 7 December 2005.

And the future: *RIBA Journal* 111:10, October 2004; *Hackney Wick Area Action Plan (Phase 1) – Masterplan*, September 2010, at http://www.hackney.gov.uk/Assets/Documents/Hackney-Wick-Phase - 1-AAP.pdf; Laurie Elks, 'The Lee Valley Regional Park: A historical perspective', *Hackney History*, Vol. 14, 2008.

Index *(Page numbers in italics refer to illustrations)*

Notes on Authors

Juliet Gardiner is a distinguished author and broadcaster. Her recent books include *The Penguin Dictionary of British History* (2000); *Wartime: Britain 1939-1945* (Headline, 2004); *The Thirties: An Intimate History* and *The Blitz: The British Under Attack* (both Harper Press, 2010). She writes and reviews for several national newspapers, and is a frequent contributor to radio programmes. She has also taken part in many television programmes, including *The 1940 House, The Edwardian Country House* and *Timewatch*. She has lived in Hackney since 1992.

David Garrard is a designation adviser at English Heritage. He has previously worked for the Victorian Society.

Matthew Green recently received a Phd from Oxford University for his thesis exploring the impact of the media in 18th-century London. He produces and presents London audio tours and is working on a popular history book, *The Lost World of the London Coffeehouse*.

Lisa Rigg is a heritage professional with experience of coordinating education and outreach projects at local and national level. In 2004, with a colleague at Time and Place Projects, she became the first winner of the Roots and Wings Award for innovative heritage provision. From 2007 to 2010 she led the work of the Hackney Society, including the editing of the award-winning *Hackney: Modern, Restored, Forgotten, Ignored*, published to mark 40 years of the Society. Since 2011 she has been managing a review of Hackney's locally listed buildings as well as developing inner London's only surviving windmill in Brixton into a visitor attraction. She has lived in Hackney since 1995.

Ann Robey is an architectural historian and heritage consultant who has written about London for over 25 years. She has worked for English Heritage and the Survey of London, as well as amenity societies, national charities and commercial clients. She has contributed to many publications and written articles on the buildings of Hackney, London's suburbs and the 18th-century Grand Tour. She is a trustee of the Heritage of London Trust.

Margaret Willes spent her working career in publishing, becoming Publisher at the National Trust. Since her retirement in 2005, she has taken up writing full time, with *Reading Matters: Five Centuries of Discovering Books* published by Yale University Press in 2008, and *Pick of the Bunch: the Story of Twelve Treasured Flowers* published by the Bodleian Library in 2009. Her latest book, *The Making of the English Gardener: Their Plants, Books and Inspiration, 1560-1660* was published by Yale in September 2011. She has lived in Hackney since 1982, and is a trustee of the Hackney Society.